INDIAN PEOPLES OF CANADA

PALMER PATTERSON

 Grolier Limited
TORONTO

FOCUS ON CANADIAN HISTORY SERIES

SERIES CONSULTANT: DESMOND MORTON

Dedicated to all the young native people of Canada and especially my grandsons, Donovan Edward and Shaughnessy Rain.

Acknowledgements: I wish to express my thanks to Mr. Ken Pearson for giving me the opportunity to participate in this series, to Mrs. Gail Heideman for typing this manuscript numerous times, and to my wife Nancy-Lou for her editorial comments and assistance.

Cover design, maps and drawings: Cheryl Trevers

Illustration credits: Glenbow Alberta Institute, cover and pages 16 and 57; Nancy-Lou Patterson, page 11; Vancouver Public Library, page 12; Metropolitan Toronto Library Board, pages 17, 31, 40; Public Archives of Canada, pages 21 (C20850), 60 (C33340), 72 (C14141); National Museums of Canada, pages 22, 33, 34, 36, 45, 48, 51, 66, 76; Alberta Archives, pages 23, 63; Department of Indian and Northern Affairs, 69, 75, 79, 80.

Canadian Cataloguing in Publication Data

Patterson, E. Palmer, 1927-
  Indian peoples of Canada

Includes index.
ISBN 0-7172-1819-8

1. Indians of North America—Canada—History.
I. Title.

E78.C2P37   971'.00497   C82-094362-2

Contents

Introduction: Indian History

Indian history is an attempt to reconstruct the past of numerous peoples, many bands, villages and small communities, and to tell their story as the history of one people. To deal in such a way with so much diversity, the historian turns to large flexible categories within which to generalize. Although the history of each community is to some extent unique, it is also possible to find valid, clearly provable, and broadly similar experiences.

In general the Canadian Indian past may be divided into five stages or phases. Since history is usually based on written sources, and since the Indians had no writing, we might call the first of these phases "prehistory"—before written records. The period of time over which this stage extends is not the same for all groups, for East Coast Micmac as for Prairie Blackfoot, or for West Coast Haida as for central Ojibwa. The beginnings of the fur trade constitute Phase Two. This was the period of first Indian-European contact, and once again there is a time difference. The eastern Indians became involved in the fur trade much earlier than the Plains or Sub-Arctic people did. Generally speaking, contact moved from east to west and from south to north.

The fur trade continues into Phase Three, which sees the Indian people losing their autonomy. At first there had been a balance of giving and receiving between the Indians and the European traders. Now the balance shifts, giving an advantage to the Europeans. The Indians are abandoning much of their native technology and substituting goods traded with the Europeans for those they used to make themselves. Dependence is the result.

Phase Four again raises the problem of chronology. Indians eventually came under government control, and by the late nineteenth century this meant reserve life, life under the Indian Act and forced assimilation. The dating for some of the key developments is fixed and the same for all—the Indian Act of 1876, for example. Reserves, on the other hand, came later in western Canada (nineteenth century) than they did in the East (late eighteenth and early nineteenth century for the most part, though the very first reserve was created in Quebec in 1637). In the northern territories, no reserves were created, although treaties of land surrender were signed and the Indians were put under the control of the Indian Act and a federal Indian administration.

Phase Five is the period of rebirth and resurgence. Again the exact dates are not rigid; some would say the inter-war years or right after World War II; others speak of 1969, the year of the federal government's "White Paper" on Indians as the key date. Precise dating is important for particular events, of course, but trends and movements sometimes have to be dated more loosely, with terms such as mid-twentieth century.

Phase I: The Shaping of the People—"Prehistory"

Canada today is a country made up of peoples from many parts of the world. Immigrants from Europe have come to form the dominant culture. It is their beliefs and customs, their languages, technology and arts that characterize Canadian society. Status and non-status Indians, Métis and Inuit—the native peoples— have become only a small part of the people called Canadians.

The name "Indian" itself is of European origin. It is the result of a mistake made by Christopher Columbus, who thought he had reached the islands of Southeast Asia known as the Indies. He had in fact reached what we call today, incorporating his error, the West Indies. Several decades passed after Columbus's voyages before enough was known about the New World to cause scholars to ask who the people already living there were and where they had come from.

The First People

The earliest archaeological remains of human beings so far found come from East Africa. Scientists believe that people spread into all parts of the world from there. Afterwards, in their various homelands, they developed their unique ways of life over long periods of time. The native Indians of Canada too developed their different cultures and languages over thousands of years. This fact is reflected in their accounts of the origins and develop- ment of their cultures in their various prehistoric homelands in Canada.

The records of earliest Indian life in Canada come from the earth. Archaeologists search for and study artifacts and physical remains—tools, weapons, houses, clothes, food—for evidence

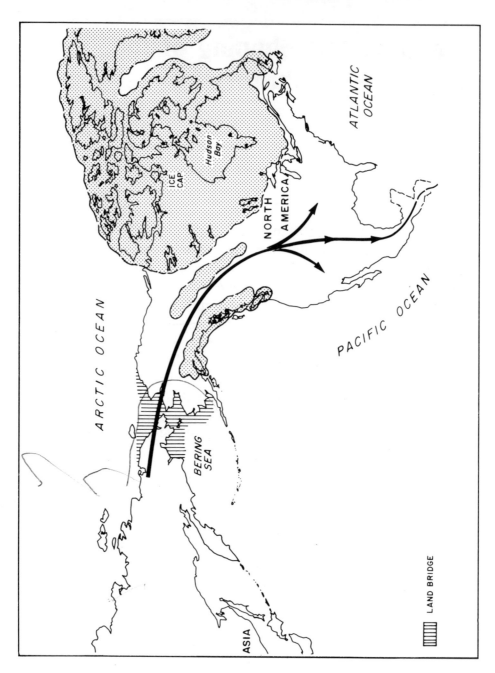

This map shows how people from Asia are believed to have come into North America thousands of years ago. The land bridge between the continents would not always have been the size shown here. It would have grown and shrunk and may even have disappeared altogether more than once as glaciers formed and melted and re-formed.

8

about these people. Their findings indicate that the first inhabitants of North America came from Asia by way of eastern Siberia and Alaska. These migrations took place over many thousands of years. They are thought to have begun thirty or forty thousand years ago, when the two continents, Asia and North America, were connected by dry land. Huge glaciers covered most of Canada, but a corridor between them allowed people to move south into what is now the United States.

By 8000 B.C., the weather had become warmer, and melting glaciers had raised the level of the sea and broken the land connection between the continents. This made it possible for people to live in parts of Canada previously covered by ice, but it made movement from Asia to North America more difficult.

One widely held theory is that there were two major migration periods with a long time gap in between. According to this theory, most Indians are descended from the people who came during the earlier migration period, while the ancestors of the Athapascan and Inuit peoples came in later migrations. Variations in physical appearance among Indians are explained as being due both to differences which existed at the time of their entry and to changes which occurred after they arrived. The various cultures which developed in the New World grew out of the cultures these people brought with them. For thousands of years they lived completely or almost completely isolated from the rest of the world. What little contact they may have had with overseas peoples is not thought to have been of major importance in shaping Indian culture in North and South America.

The Paleo-Indians or Big-Game Hunters

The earliest inhabitants of North America lived at a time (the Paleolithic, or Old Stone Age) when stone was widely used for utensils, tools and weapons. Wood, bone, horn and hide were also used for these purposes, but these materials decay and so have not often survived. Freezing has preserved a few fragments, but not enough to indicate how commonly they were used.

Our information about the Old Stone Age people comes from stones, tools and weapons found at their ancient camping sites or at places where they got the stone which they shaped into spear points or cutting and hammering tools. Rarely, an animal skeleton may be found with a spearhead in the bone. By analyzing the amount of carbon content in vegetable or animal matter found with stone objects, scientists can calculate how long ago these people lived.

The population of Canada 400 years ago is thought to have been about two hundred and fifty thousand. Estimates for 10,000 or 20,000 years ago are much smaller. These estimates are made by counting the number of sites found, by studying the artifacts found, by analysing the patterns of making a living and by observing more recent people who lived or still live by similar means.

The earliest people are called Paleo-Indian. They based their subsistence on hunting for big game, such as the mammoth, bison and caribou, and to a lesser extent on fishing and gathering edible plants. They relied on hand-chipped stone tools and hunting weapons such as scrapers, knives and spearheads. Their small communities were probably composed of related people: parents, children, grandparents, uncles and aunts and their children. The size of the group might vary according to the season and the amount of food available.

Archaic and Woodland Cultures

As the glaciers began to melt and retreat northward, people, animals and plants moved northward too. The population at this time was very small, but the warming climate brought more and more changes. By about 8000 B.C. a greater variety of food was available and a new era, known to scientists as the Archaic period, was beginning. Its culture soon extended across southern Canada from the East to the Prairies. Archaeologists find more sites from this period than from the previous Big-Game Hunting period. The sites are larger and richer in material, indicating a larger population and a higher standard of living. The people now hunted deer, bear, elk and smaller game and birds. They caught fish and shellfish and gathered nuts, seeds and plants. Regional differences began to develop in this widespread culture, though there remained a general similarity due to the rapidity with which it spread.

By 1000 B.C. Archaic culture in eastern North America had evolved into the early Woodland culture. In this period we see

Although the Indians had no writing, a few groups did record events by means of symbolic figures carved or painted on large rocks. These are called petroglyphs when carved, pictographs when painted. The above petroglyph was found near Peterborough, Ontario.

gradual change rather than mass migrations of people, as well as the gradual spreading of culture traits and their absorption by stable populations. Generally, the spreading of culture traits moved from south to north, with local variations. Although there was no major break with the past, two new features appeared which spread from the midwestern United States—pottery and ceremonial burials. Pottery is a useful find for archaeologists since differences of size, shape, colour, style and use assist in describing the culture and in showing changes from one period to another. Copper tools also appeared towards the end of the period.

Woodland cultures were still dominant through most of Canada when the Indians first met the Europeans.

West Coast Cultures

In far-western Canada, distinct cultures emerged on the Pacific coast and in the plateau area about eight thousand years ago.

11

They developed from an ancient culture, Old Cordilleran, which resembled that of the Big-Game Hunters but had certain characteristics of its own. Over several thousand more years of adaptation and change, the coastal peoples developed the distinctive lifestyle which evolved into the West Coast culture that was still there in historic times.

In the area that is the homeland of the Tsimshian people, archeologists have found evidence of a culture 5000 years old. This culture changed gradually, without any sharp breaks, as the people grew more efficient in the use of local material resources—trees, sea life, wild foods—and as they improved their tools and weapons. By A.D. 500 it had assumed a form recognizable as the West Coast culture of historic times. Art styles, burial customs and objects found in graves, the size, location and wealth of houses, all show the signs of the rich status-and-rank-conscious

The totem poles of Skidegate. The huge carved poles of the Haida are no doubt the best-known feature of West Coast culture. Each Haida house was entered by a small doorway cut through the base of the tall housepole. The figures carved on the pole represented the owner's crests and incidents in his or his family's history. There might also be two shorter poles at the front corners of the house, and nearby would be raised the mortuary posts which served as tombs for the dead. These might be plain or carved depending on the wealth of the person.

society of the Tsimshian seen by the Europeans in the early nineteenth century. Some of the villages had occupied the same site for several thousand years. Their middens, or garbage dumps, have provided useful material for archaeologists to study in reconstructing Tsimshian pre-history.

Ways of Living: Sharing the World

Life in a small community called for care and thoughtfulness in dealing with others. The members of the community lived together very closely, intensely at times. It was important that their behaviour be such as to preserve individual feelings, rights and interests and to preserve also the unity of the group. Without rules and customs to control behaviour, stresses could tear the group apart, threatening everyone's survival. Rivalries, differences of ability and temperament, of age and sex, had to be submerged for the good of the whole.

Rules and regulations were not written down because there was no writing, but they were passed on by word of mouth. We do not know what the oldest rules were, but we do know about the customs of more recent communities of hunters. It seems likely that the rules of earlier times would have been similar. There might have been rules governing the way people spoke to each other, or forbidding speaking between certain categories of people except on special occasions. On the other hand, an individual might have been allowed to express an opinion without interruption or contradiction regardless of whether or not others agreed. Children were perhaps subject to little restraint on their behaviour and yet expected to contribute to the group at an early age. All of these customs have been observed in historic times among one or more native tribes.

Everyone was expected to make a contribution. Men hunted and fished, women gathered wild foods and prepared meat and hides. Children gathered water and wood and learned not only to use the tools and weapons of their culture but also to make them. Although there was some trading, most of the things used were made and shared within the family or community. A person who was especially skilled at a certain activity might make items for others. Cooperation was essential. Private property was likely to be non-material: a story, a song or a dance.

Anger and violence were a danger to the group. Most Canadian Indians were hunters, and a delicate balance had to be maintained between the animal and plant life and the size of the hunting group. The whole community might be destroyed if some part of it was in opposition to another part.

If a member grew very discontented, it was possible to leave and join a nearby group, or band, probably containing relatives. One could also break away to form one's own band with a few friends and their families. But expulsion from the group was severe punishment. The chief was a man who shared, and his authority came not from a "badge of office," but from his skill as a hunter and arbritrator and from his generosity in giving his own property to others. Most people would not readily leave such a person.

Difficult circumstances—cold, food shortage, danger from animals or nature—had to be met with calm, self-control and perseverance. Knowledge of the habits, food and location of the animals hunted was essential, as was skill in making weapons, tools and utensils. Religious attitudes, knowledge and behaviour could also determine success or failure at the hunt. Spiritual preparation and supernatural aid might be called for. Not everyone was successful all the time, and it was sharing that ensured survival in the long term.

Agricultural Tribes and Tribes of the West Coast

Some time before the arrival of the Europeans, a branch of the Woodland culture in parts of eastern Canada began to cultivate the land. This branch developed into the agricultural Iroquoian-speaking peoples. These groups also hunted, and the two tasks,

These drawings show only two of the great variety of fish weir used by Canadian Indians. Above, one type of Nootka salmon weir. As the salmon swam upriver to spawn, they were stopped by the weir and forced into the conical traps placed in the V formed by the weir and the river bank. Below, a tidal weir used by the Indians of the Atlantic coast. Fish feeding at high tide in the shallow water near the shore would swim along the fence and into the enclosure. As the tide receded, most would be trapped and the fishermen could simply scoop them up.

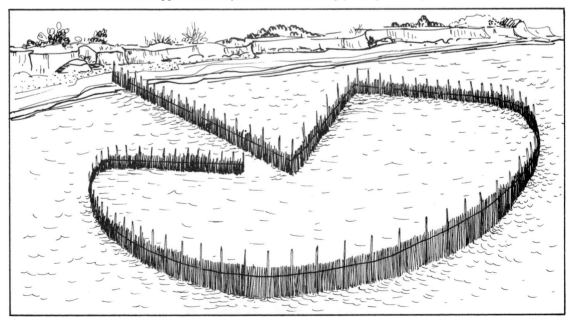

hunting and farming, were divided between men and women. The men did the hunting and the women looked after all aspects of raising the crops, from tilling the soil to harvesting.

Farming provided a greater and more stable food supply than did hunting. As a result agricultural groups were larger than those that lived entirely by hunting and gathering. They were also settled in villages which sometimes reached populations of a thousand. Settled populations could have more material possessions, and this meant there were greater differences of wealth and prestige within a community. The Hurons and their neighbours the Tobacco (so named from their main crop) and the Neutrals (from their efforts, unsuccessful, to stay out of the Huron-Iroquois War) were Canada's main agricultural tribes by the early seventeenth century.

On the coast of British Columbia the annual runs of fish and the supply of shellfish and sea mammals made it possible for the people there to live in settled villages for part of the year. This

Life was harsh for most Indians, but they managed to find some time for play. Shown here is a group of Sioux involved in a game of lacrosse. Many tribes played a version of this game, which the Ojibwa called baggatawy. *There were variations from tribe to tribe in the length and shape of the stick, the composition of the ball and the number of players per team (there could be as many as 200). But the game was always fast and rugged and often ended in serious injuries to some participants.*

Gambling and guessing games using fruit stones, painted pieces of bone, sticks and straws were popular among almost all Canadian Indians. Here a group of Sioux women play with dice made of peachstones.

peculiar richness of uncultivated resources produced large villages of several hundred people, making coastal groups unique among non-agricultural tribes. They developed an elaborate culture of ceremony and ceremonial objects as well as ranks and classes within their society. Like the farming peoples, they were the hub of important trading and trade routes. Their languages and customs were taken up by their trading partners, and their cultural influence, like that of the agricultural tribes, spread out to neighbouring peoples of differing languages, cultures, and circumstances.

Beliefs and Values: Living in a Sacred World

There were no sharp divisions between humans, nature, spirits, spiritual force, the living and the non-living. All were linked together and intertwined. Animals and plants were not the servants or humans the masters. Indians saw themselves as one of the elements in the world, not the lords of creation. They called upon the animals and the plants to assist them, to sacrifice their lives for human survival.

In this view of the world, called animism, all elements in nature—humans, animals, plants, rocks, rivers, lakes, stars, rain, the sun and moon—have souls or spiritual force. Some writers have called this a kind of spiritual electricity. The spirits of these elements or a portion of this spiritual force could be contacted and appealed to by prayer, fasting, meditation and sacrifice in order to gain supernatural support, whether for the hunt or for making a canoe or for gathering roots or raising crops.

When a woman cuts the roots of a young cedar tree she prays, "Look at me, friend! I come to ask for your dress, for you have come to take pity on us; for there is nothing for which you can not be used, because it is your way that there is nothing for which we cannot use you, for you are really willing to give us your dress. I come to beg you for this, long lifemaker, for I am going to make a basket for lily roots out of you. I pray, friend, not to feel angry with me on account of what I am going to do to you, and I beg you, friend, to tell your friends about what I ask of you. Take care, friend! Keep sickness away from me, so that I may not be killed by sickness or in war, O friend!"

KWAKIUTL WOMAN'S PRAYER
TRANSLATED BY FRANZ BOAS (1921)

Generally speaking, everyone could have contact with the supernatural, but some people had greater skills. These were the result of special relations with a spirit helper, a kind of "guardian angel." The spirit helper came to the individual after prayer, fasting and visions which usually began in adolescence and remained with the person for life. Contact between a person and his or her spirit helper was made periodically for renewal and strengthening of powers. Spiritual exercises such as prayer and fasting were repeated. Not all of these ways of obtaining supernatural help are found in all tribes.

Special respect for the animal prey might be called for. Thanks and recognition of its sacrifice of its life to feed humans might take the form of special disposal of the bones or other parts of the animal. Among the Kwakiutl, the bear was treated with an elaborate ritual before being eaten. The Nishga called the eulachon, or candlefish, "salvation fish" because it came in the spring to restock their food supply after the winter. Some tribes practised "first fruits" ceremonies: West Coast Indians, for example, celebrated the arrival of the first salmon. Healing and cur-

All tribes danced, usually in a circle and to the beat of drums. Although they sometimes danced simply for pleasure, most dances had religious significance. The dancers in this photograph are calling back the eclipsed moon.

ing illnesses also required spiritual help as well as technical skill.

Sounds and sights were interpreted as messages from spirits. The sounds of birds or animals were messages which gave knowledge and control if properly understood. Individuals could also receive knowledge and power through their dreams. Dreams and visions sometimes provided warnings, telling of coming events or situations to be sought or avoided. They sometimes suggested new religious ceremonies or forms of conduct. The sensitive and instructed person was thus given the necessary edge to survive and to prosper.

The person who was not in proper relation with the supernatural could not expect to be successful in a regular way. Ill treatment of an animal might be punished by a poor hunt or catch. Brutality or cruelty to other forms of life could bring punishment to an entire community if no steps were taken to correct the behaviour. Natural disasters were sometimes interpreted as such punishment. In these cases specialists in dealing with spirits and spiritual forces were called in to find out what had gone wrong and what could be done about it. These were the medicine men or shamans found in all communities.

Among the Ojibwa and other Algonkian-speaking Indians, spiritual force was called *manitou*. The Great Manitou was the Great Spirit and was believed to be the creator God and the preserver of humankind. A person in need might call upon the Great Spirit or upon the spiritual force which dwelt in some particular element. Ideas about the Great Spirit continued to develop into modern times.

Among the Hurons medicine men called *oki* controlled supernatural power, *onadaki*. The Iroquois, some of whom settled in southern Ontario in the late eighteenth century, believed that people, plants and animals were created out of the supernatural power, *orenda*.

The Sioux, who moved back and forth across the border between Canada and the United States, as did many native people, called the supernatural power *wakan*. Wakan Tonka was the Great Mystery, God, and was sometimes prayed to as "Grandfather."

Everyday life and religion were deeply intermixed among Indians. Most did not, however, have church organizations with clergy, nor did they have elaborately developed bodies of religious laws, creeds and theologies. Belief and worship were more often personal, though fitted into the beliefs of the community.

Among the Ojibwa there was, nevertheless, a religious society, the Midewiwin, which had framed a system of beliefs and practices. It was open to those who would accept the teaching and the step-by-step training of the society. Membership was by initiation, and members gained spiritual knowledge not available to the uninitiated. Only members could perform the sacred ceremonies of the Midewiwin.

The Potlatch

Organizations that mixed religion and social status flourished among the Indians of coastal British Columbia. Initiation required having a vision, but in some cases only the upper class could have the visions which permitted membership in these ceremonial organizations. The West Coast people lived mainly on fish, clams, oysters, crab and sea mammals. They spent the spring and summer in temporary homes on the riverbanks or seashore collecting the food supplies that would see them through the year. In the autumn they returned to their permanent villages, where until spring they carried on their rich ceremonial life with costumes, masks, songs and dances. Wealthy people held great feasts and gave away property as a sign of some important change in the rank, title or other status of some member of their family. To collect the food and goods for feasting and gift-giving, a person might take months or even years and call upon the immediate family and related families to contribute. This particular form of ceremony was called a potlatch.

The Nishga Tradition of the Nass River Land Plain

"The river did not always flow where it does now. It flowed along by the base of the mountains on the farther side of the valley some miles away. It was there the people were encamped when the Nak-Nok of the mountain became angry and the firestone flowed down. They were all busy in catching, cleaning, and cutting up the salmon, to dry in the smoke. Whilst they were thus engaged, some of the boys were amusing themselves in catching salmon, and cutting openings in their backs, in which they inserted long, narrow stones. Then, setting them free in the water, as the salmon swam near the surface, the boys clapped their hands and called them finback whales.

While they were thus enjoying their cruel sport, the ground began to tremble, and suddenly the mountain vomited forth fire and smoke."

W. H. COLLISON
IN THE WAKE OF THE WAR CANOE (1915)

The Shaking Tent Ceremony

Among many of the Indians of eastern Canada a small wooden framework was built and enclosed by a wall of bark. A medicine man then entered this lodge and was tied up. While spectators waited outside, the tent began to shake and the man inside talked to and received messages from the spirit world. Sometimes, it was believed, he flew out for a while, perhaps in the form of a bird.

Later the medicine man emerged from the tent free of his bonds and possessing information or advice from his supernatural sources. Through this Shaking Tent ceremony, he might deal with problems ranging from healing the sick to finding lost objects.

The Sun Dance

In the summer, the Indians of the Prairies, such as the Blackfoot, Sarsi, Plains Cree and Plains Ojibwa, held a ceremony known as the Sun Dance. The events lasted a week or so and usually began with a buffalo hunt because a good supply of meat was required to feed the many people who gathered to join in or watch. The ceremony contained parts from the religious practices of several

Ojibwa Shaking Tent ceremony. The medicine man is already inside the tent. Soon, while his assistant beats a drum outside, the tent will begin to shake and voices will be heard as he communicates with the spirit world.

The Sun Dance was the Plains Indians' most important religious ritual. Putting up the enclosure was an important part of the ceremony and one in which many people took part. The central pole was chosen after solemn prayer, and a fixed order had to be observed in adding the other poles.

tribes who met regularly and borrowed from one another. Those who took part in the actual dance gazed at the sun or at a central pole inside a large circular enclosure as they danced. They took neither food nor water and continued dancing hour after hour for two to four days. The dance was intended as a personal sacrifice to fulfill a promise or pledge in exchange for supernatural help received or asked for. Gathering food, building the enclosure and bringing in and setting up the central Sun Dance pole were all regarded as important religious participation in the ceremony.

The particular form of the Sun Dance ceremony differed from one group to another and changed over the years as well. The full ceremony consisted of twenty-eight parts, including the dance, but no tribe practised all twenty-eight. The central theme was the prayer for supernatural aid. The federal government, focusing on the elements of self-torture which some tribes practised as part of the ceremony, outlawed it in the late nineteenth century. The potlatch too was outlawed. Not until more than fifty years later, in 1951, were these ceremonies again legally performed.

23

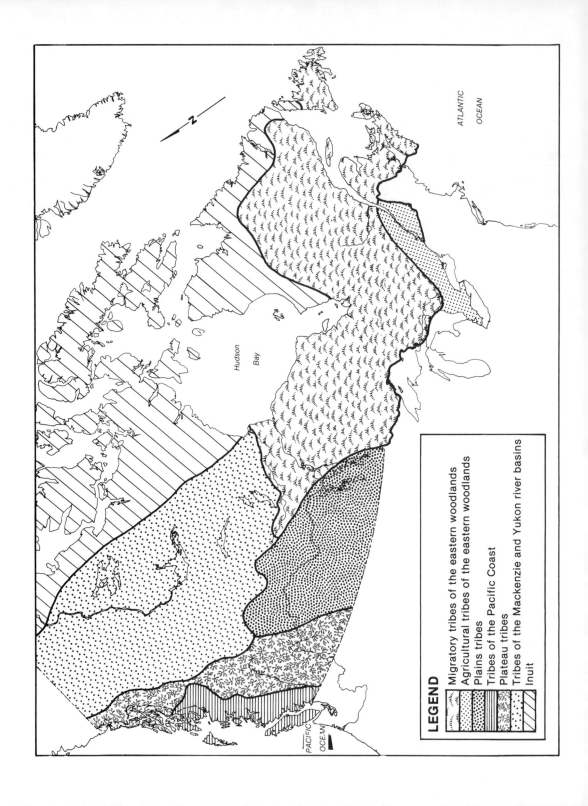

LEGEND

Migratory tribes of the eastern woodlands
Agricultural tribes of the eastern woodlands
Plains tribes
Tribes of the Pacific Coast
Plateau tribes
Tribes of the Mackenzie and Yukon river basins
Inuit

N

ATLANTIC OCEAN

Hudson Bay

PACIFIC OCEAN

The Sweat Lodge

Among the Algonkian, a more personal form of religious exercise was the use of the sweat lodge. Inside a little hut or tent, a fire was built to heat stones over which the occupant sprinkled water. The sweating which resulted was thought to purify the body and the spirit and to make the person more ready to be in communion · with the physical-spiritual world.

Languages and Cultural Areas

The study of the languages of the Canadian Indians shows that some are similar to each other, while others are not related. The languages are therefore grouped into language families.

Tribes which have related languages are not necessarily closely related in other ways, however. The study of the lifestyles, customs and beliefs of the various tribes has resulted in the proposing of "culture areas." The tribes of a culture area are said to bear a close cultural ressemblance to each other although they may speak widely different languages and be of different language families.

Stability and Change

Language and culture groupings can be useful ways of studying Indians, but they must not be thought of as rigid and permanent pigeonholes. Even the most ancient peoples in Canada were not unchanging in their way of life. Change was slower before 1600 than it was after, but it was taking place. As objects were traded over hundreds, even thousands of kilometres, borrowing, trading and visiting introduced people to new ideas and new tools and equipment. Marriage or kidnapping from one group to another could also create variety and differences within a community.

Internal changes could take place too through creative variation in making objects for use. Stories, legends and other oral traditions had individual versions. Dreams and visions were individual experiences and taught individual skills.

Culture areas of Canada. Each area was inhabited by tribes who had a similar way of life. The differences from one area to another were mainly the result of centuries of adaptation to different physical environments.

Linguistic Families and Related Languages of Canadian Indians

Some of the languages included in this list are no longer spoken. Beothuk died out with the extinction of its speakers; as the Huron, Neutral and Nicola were absorbed into surrounding tribes, their languages too were lost. A Huron community still exists at Lorette, Quebec, but its members are now all French speaking. Other languages, such as those of the Iroquois Confederacy, were not spoken in Canada until after the arrival of the Europeans.

ALGONKIAN

Abenaki
Algonkin
Blackfoot
Cree
Delaware
Malecite
Micmac
Montagnais
Naskapi
Ottawa
Potawatomi

ATHAPASKAN

Beaver
Carrier
Chilcotin
Chipewyan
Dogrib
Hare
Kaska
Kutchin
Loucheux
Nahani
Nicola
Sarsi
Sekani
Slave
Tagish
Tahltan
Yellowknife

BEOTHUKAN

Beothuk

HAIDAN

Haida

IROQUOIAN

Huron
Languages of Iroquois Confederacy
    Cayuga
    Mohawk
    Oneida
    Onondaga
    Seneca
Neutral

KOOTENAYAN

Kootenay

SALISHAN

Bella Coola
Comox
Halkomelen (Cowichan)
Lillooet
Sechelt
Shuswap
Squamish
Straits
Thompson

SIOUAN

Assiniboine
Dakota

TLINGIT

Inland Tlingit

TSIMSHIAN

Coast Tsimshian
Gitksan
Nishga

WAKASHAN

Haisla
Heiltsuk
Kwakiutl
Nootka

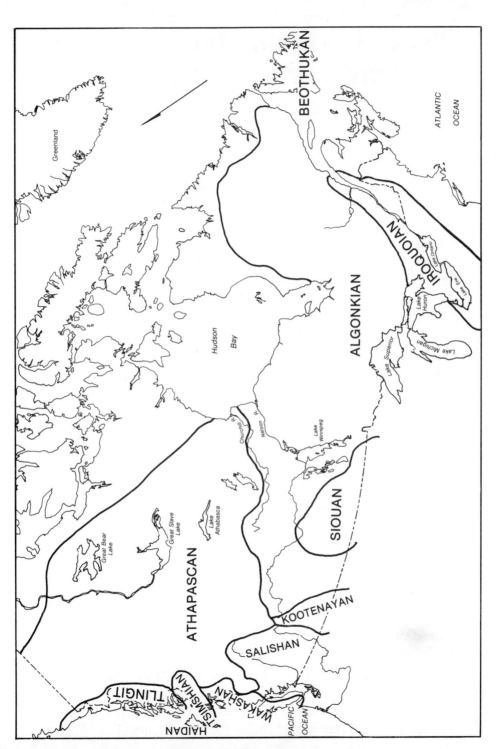

BEOTHUKAN

ATLANTIC
OCEAN

Greenland

IROQUOIAN

Lake Ontario

Lake Erie

Lake Huron

ALGONKIAN

Lake Michigan

Lake Superior

Hudson
Bay

Churchill R.

Nelson R.

Lake
Winnipeg

SIOUAN

Great Bear
Lake

Great Slave
Lake

Lake
Athabasca

ATHAPASCAN

KOOTENAYAN

SALISHAN

WAKASHAN

TLINGIT

TSIMSHIAN

HAIDAN

PACIFIC
OCEAN

Phase II: Turning Into "Indians"—Partnership and Cooperation

The first Indians to see the Europeans arrive in Canada were eastern coastal people, perhaps the Beothuk of Newfoundland or the Micmac of New Brunswick or the Iroquoian peoples along the St. Lawrence River. The arrival of the Europeans changed Indian life and the change grew more rapid as contact increased.

The name Canada is Indian, probably from the St. Lawrence Iroquoians' word *kanata*, meaning a village or community. Others, including the Cree, have also claimed the word for their languages.

The Beothuk

Most of what is now known about the Beothuk comes from archaeological information and from the drawings and accounts of a young Beothuk woman called Shanawdithit.

Like most Canadian Indians, the Beothuk lived as hunters and gatherers. Their food changed with the seasons, and they moved in a regular annual cycle in order to secure it. In spring and summer they hunted the animals and birds of the shore and collected birds' eggs. During the winter months they hunted inland game, including the caribou.

The Beothuk may have seen and even had occasional contact with Vikings around the year 1000. There was a Viking settlement on the northern tip of Newfoundland, at L'Anse aux Meadows, but it died out long before John Cabot cruised the coastal waters of eastern Canada. Fishing ships from Portugal, Spain, France and the British Isles may have visited Canadian shores as early as the mid-fifteenth century. If so, by the time Jacques Cartier came

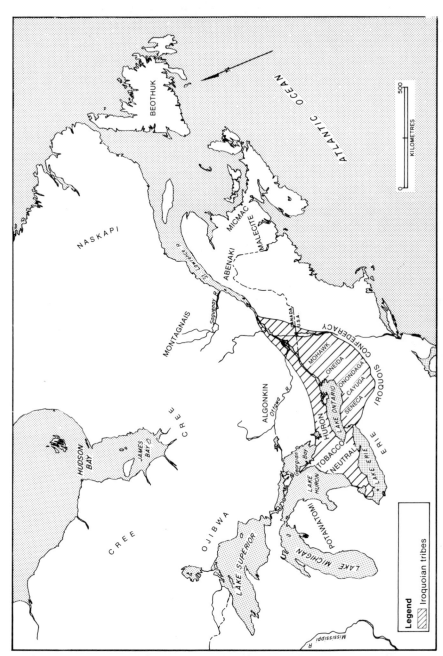

Approximate location of the main tribes of eastern Canada around the time of Cartier's arrival in the 1530s.

up the St. Lawrence in the 1530s some Indians may have been in contact with Europeans for two or three generations. Such contact would, however, have been sporadic and probably rare.

Beothuk contact, whenever it occurred, took a distinctive turn. Perhaps they resented the intruders who fished and hunted in their territory, who cut trees and scoured the land for resources. A long history of conflict, disease, raids, kidnappings and killings developed. In the eighteenth century efforts were made to establish peaceful relations, but they were hindered by mistrust and suspicion. It was too late for the pattern to be changed. By the early nineteenth century the Beothuk had dwindled to a handful of people fleeing and hiding from the Europeans. Shanawdithit was, as far as anyone can determine, the last of the Beothuk. She died in 1829. The lack of cooperation and shared interests between Beothuk and Europeans had led to the destruction of a people and their culture.

The St. Lawrence Iroquoians

In the 1530s and the 1540s Iroquoian-speaking peoples lived along the shore of the St. Lawrence. They combined farming and hunting and lived in palisaded villages. At two of their settlements, Stadacona (Quebec City area) and Hochelaga (Montreal area) they met Jacques Cartier and supplied him with information about their culture. They also told him about more prosperous peoples to the west. During the second of three encounters with Cartier and his men, the Indians saved the Europeans' lives by introducing them to a native medicine which cured scurvy, a disease from which many of the crew members were suffering. The Europeans repaid this kindness by kidnapping several members of the host community and taking them to France. Some of these people never returned. Donnaconna, a chief of Stadacona, died in France; his two sons were more fortunate—they eventually returned to their home.

During the decades from the 1540s to the early seventeenth century the St. Lawrence Iroquois ceased to occupy the area. We have no real information as to why, but certainly the half-century had brought changes to the people. Europeans had established permanent trading posts, and their ships had begun to come upriver regularly to trade for furs. Beaver hats were becoming fashionable in Europe, and the demand for furs, especially beaver pelts, was increasing rapidly.

Perhaps the people sought a new home as pressures in the area mounted. Perhaps some were killed in warfare for beaver territories or were driven out or absorbed by neighbouring Algonkian-speaking peoples who moved into their territory. In the late sixteenth and early seventeenth centuries, at least two groups moved westward and attached themselves to the Hurons on the southeast shore of Georgian Bay. Another explanation offered for the disappearance of the Iroquois from the St. Lawrence region was that they found themselves too far north to practise their type of agriculture successfully. It was probably some combination of these factors that led them to abandon their homeland. Whatever their reasons, they were more fortunate than the Beothuk. They survived because they had a large interior area in which to retire and kinsmen, the Hurons, to receive them.

Algonkians: Montagnais

The people who greeted Samuel de Champlain in the early seventeenth century were Algonkian speakers who lived by hunting,

Micmac women in their lodge. Note the salmon hanging to dry and the distinctive caps the women are wearing. These and all articles of Micmac clothing were decorated with symbolic designs embroidered onto them with dyed porcupine quills or moose hair.

fishing and gathering. They followed a seasonal migration pattern in their search for food and did not live in settled villages. Their skills and knowledge made them successful trading partners. On the Lower St. Lawrence, the Algonkians were coming regularly each summer to trade with European ships by 1580. By 1600 Algonkian bands in the area between the Saguenay and St. Maurice rivers were acting as middlemen for interior bands. They had taken control of the river routes and demanded payment from interior peoples wishing to come to the St. Lawrence to trade. One of them, the Montagnais (Mountaineer) Indians, may have contributed to the uprooting of the St. Lawrence Iroquois.

In 1603 some of these people met Champlain, and in 1609 they and he made a famous raid against the Iroquois of New York, who were also trying to control the traffic in furs. The Montagnais thus became friends, allies and trading partners of the French. They accepted the Christian religion brought to them by missionaries and introduced the Hurons to the fur trade. Some of the Hurons, however, may already have had trade connections from their earlier residence at Hochelaga or Stadacona.

The lure of the fur trade was very strong, and competition grew fierce between the Montagnais and the Iroquois of New York (the then five-nations League of the Iroquois—Mohawk, Oneida, Onondaga, Cayuga, and Seneca). In 1637, to protect themselves from increasingly bold raids by the Iroquois, some Montagnais consented to move onto the first Indian reserve in Canada at Sillery, near Quebec City. By this time they were dependent on their French allies for European manufactured goods. Their population declined as a result of epidemic diseases introduced from Europe, and commercial fur trapping passed deeper into the continent's interior.

Although the more interior Montagnais were involved in the fur trade, they did not become totally dependent on commercial activities. Hunting for food and gathering remained important to their livelihood. Their even more remote neighbours, the Naskapi, lived with even less change. They accepted some tools and weapons from the French but remained essentially small communities of hunters. In fact, the Naskapi of the early twentieth century lived basically as the Montagnais had done several centuries earlier.

Model of a Huron village. All the agricultural tribes of the Great Lakes–St. Lawrence region lived in more or less similar villages, some of which contained as many as forty or fifty longhouses. These were covered in cedar or elm bark and shared by several related families, sometimes as many as twenty. Each village also had a somewhat larger village longhouse for meetings and ceremonies. Every ten or fifteen years, when firewood ran out or when the land within easy reach of the village was exhausted and no longer produced good crops, the village would be abandoned and another built at a new location.

Hurons and Iroquois

Farther west the Huron Indians were organized as a confederation of four tribes. Their central location put them in easy reach of Indians all around them, and they became the key people in a widespread trading system that included the Ottawa and other Algonkian speakers to the north and the Tobacco Indians to the south. Their agricultural products, such as corn and hemp, were exchanged for the fish and furs of their neighbours. By the early seventeenth century the Hurons had been drawn into the fur trade of the French, and their importance in it can be seen from the fact that the language of trade and diplomacy was the Huron language. They dominated the trade and prevented independent trading by their partners, the Tobacco and Neutral.

The Hurons suffered a fifty percent decline in their population in the 1630s as a result of a smallpox epidemic introduced through their European trading partners. Pro- and anti-French factions developed, and they debated future relations between

Inside the longhouse there were sleeping platforms along each side with racks for storage above them. Ears of corn were hung from the crosspoles to dry. A row of fires, each shared by the family on either side, ran down the centre. Although there were openings in the roof for ventilation, the smoke from the fires hung heavy inside the lodge in wintertime, and eye trouble was a very common problem.

themselves and the French representatives, the Jesuit missionaries. These men, the most famous of whom was Father Jean de Brébeuf, and their assistants (*donneés*) had begun to come into Huronia in the mid-1630s.

A further disaster awaited the Hurons in the 1640s. Many had accepted the French trading alliance and some had been converted to the new religion. The population had levelled off. Now the Iroquois demanded that the Hurons share the fur trade. The French opposed such a move because it would redirect much of the trade from its St. Lawrence route (in French control) to a Hudson River route (in Dutch control). The Iroquois tried diplomacy and a fur trade treaty, but these arrangements broke down. Factions were again at work in Huronia. The Hurons most strongly linked to the fur trade were the most pro-French and perhaps also the most likely to be Christians.

The Iroquois turned to war in order to get furs, and they

adopted a style of warfare very different from the fighting which had taken place before the Europeans came. Between 1648 and 1651 they attacked first the Hurons and then the Tobacco and Neutrals with massive forces. Many died in these attacks and many others were scattered. Those sympathetic to the Iroquois joined their cultural cousins and removed to New York. Others joined related tribes, the Susquehanna (Andastes) and the Erie. Still others moved northwestward to their allies and trading partners the Ottawa and re-formed themselves as a people linked to the Ojibwa, Ottawa and Potawatomi (the Council of Three Fires) of the Upper Great Lakes.

Many Christian Hurons were led by their Jesuit pastors and teachers to Christian Island in Georgian Bay. There they spent a winter of starvation after their crops failed. The survivors migrated to Quebec City, finally settling at Lorette. The Iroquois built several villages on the north shore of Lake Ontario (one later became Toronto) and hunted throughout southern Ontario.

Those refugees who fled northwest continued to be part of the fur trade system, which had by now reached the Upper Great Lakes. The Iroquois were still determined to get control of the trade and raided all the way to Manitoulin Island, and beyond to Sault Ste. Marie. The need to escape them as well as the abundance of fish and the westward movement of the fur trade drew various peoples to the shores of Lake Superior. There, villages composed of members of a variety of tribes soon emerged.

Most of these people were employed in the fur trade as hunters, middlemen, canoers, freighters, interpreters, guides, food suppliers, or military allies. They were dependent on the trade and on European goods. As they mixed together, their cultures blended to some extent creating a greater similarity among them. Most of these people were linked to the French trading interest.

The Ojibwa

One of these peoples, the Ojibwa (also known as Chippewa or Nishnawbe), originally centered in the Sault Ste. Marie area, spread in all directions as they too were drawn into the trade. Some travelled to Wisconsin and Minnesota where they eventually established family connections with the Sioux as well as trade links which lasted from the late seventeenth century well into the

Two types of Ojibwa wigwam. Both could be put up in an hour or less and dismantled in minutes. The conical lodge was the typical dwelling of all the non-agricultural tribes of eastern Canada. Depending on the region and its climate, the framework of poles was covered with skins, bark or rush mats. Skins were preferred in cold, dry areas, bark (which dried faster) in areas which received a lot of rain or wet snow. Because frozen bark was awkward to roll up for moving, it was often replaced by rush mats in the wintertime. The bark-covered, dome-shaped lodge on the right was also common among the Ojibwa and Cree of eastern Canada. A lodge of the same shape but covered with skins was used by the Kutchin Indians of the Yukon River basin.

eighteenth. Others moved south, north and west. By the early eighteenth century, some Ojibwa had migrated into Southern Ontario, where they clashed with the Iroquois and occupied most of the area.

Ojibwa and Ottawa groups were steady allies of the French and remained so throughout the Seven Years' War, the final struggle between Britain and France in North America. Their encampments were to be found throughout the Upper Great Lakes, and they fought against other Indians in the area who allied with the British. An Ottawa-French captain, Charles Michel de Langlade, led Ottawa and Ojibwa forces into the Ohio valley against the British-allied Miami Chief, Old Briton. An Ottawa chief, Pontiac, led a pro-French attack against more than a dozen English forts in 1763, at the end of the war. Ojibwa friendship with the French led many of them to join Pontiac's rising. It was an Ojibwa, Chief Minnewehna, who led the capture of Fort Michilimackinac. Another Ojibwa involved in that event, Wawatam, helped to protect and care for an English trader, Alexander Henry, captured at the fort. Much of what we know of Ojibwa daily life in the mid-eighteenth century comes from Henry's diary of his year with Wawatam's family.

Mamongesedo was yet another Ojibwa chief who fought for the French at Quebec in 1759. He was a practical man, and after the British victory, he and his son Waubojeeg were won to British friendship by Sir William Johnson, the superintendent of Indian Affairs in the northern colonies.

Despite migration, population decline and much cultural change, the majority of the Indians did not lose their own cultural heritage. They had absorbed much from each other and from the Europeans; they had changed and often suffered due to change. But their family, clan or other kinship ties were flexible and strong. Waubojeeg explained to Sir William Johnson the freedom and individualism of his people, the Ojibwa. He would try to persuade his followers to become friends of the British, he said, but he had no power to force them. The Indian system of government was based on consent, persuasion and the good reputation of the chief. This was the tradition and it continued to operate.

The Cree

The Cree, another major Indian tribe of Ontario, were also affected by events stemming from the Europeans and the fur trade. They hunted along the southern shores of Hudson Bay and James Bay and in the adjacent interior areas. Those along the coast were known as the Swampy Cree and later sometimes as the Home Indians. Those deeper in the interior were the Woodland Cree. Like the Ojibwa and Ottawa they spoke a language of the Algonkian family. They lived in bands which varied in size according to the food supply, which in turn was related to the seasons.

The Cree became involved in the fur trade in the mid-seventeenth century, but their participation in it and its influence on them increased late in the century. In 1670 the Hudson's Bay Company sent its first trading expedition to Hudson Bay, and within a few years it began building forts and trading posts at convenient river mouths. The Cree suddenly found themselves on the doorstep of a new trade route.

They too became trappers, middlemen, and company employees. Over the next hundred years or more of contact they expanded their role in the fur trade. In the late eighteenth century the Hudson's Bay Company began to build posts in the interior, away from the shores of the Bay. Some Cree began to hunt buffalo on the prairies to supply meat in the form of pemmican to the Europeans at these posts. They took to the horse which had only recently (about 1750) come to be used by Indians already living in the open country. These people became the Plains Cree. This step shows the adaptability of the Cree, but their specialization as meat suppliers led to a dependency on the buffalo.

The Plains Indians

The Blackfoot peoples of the Prairies—the Siksika or Blackfoot proper, the Kainai or Blood and the Piegan—became rivals and enemies of the Plains Cree as they competed for buffalo and horses. They developed a kind of feuding which included stealing horses from each other and attacking each other's camps. The Blackfoot had acquired the horse from the Shoshoni, who lived to the south and west of them and then migrated from central Saskatchewan into southern Alberta.

The Plains Cree allied themselves to the Siouan-speaking Assiniboine, who had suffered drastic population reduction as a result of epidemic diseases brought by the Europeans. Cree-Assiniboine trade extended from Hudson Bay to the upper Missouri River.

These days in the late eighteenth and early nineteenth centuries were later looked upon as the golden era of the Plains Indians. They had the advantage of the use of horses and some European technology, but their culture was intact and adapting at its own pace. Disease had destroyed many, but increased prosperity had aided others, especially the Cree, who became the centre of a widespread trade network. The Cree language was the universal language of trade in the Prairie Provinces.

The Métis

The Métis are an ethnic group native to Canada, a people of

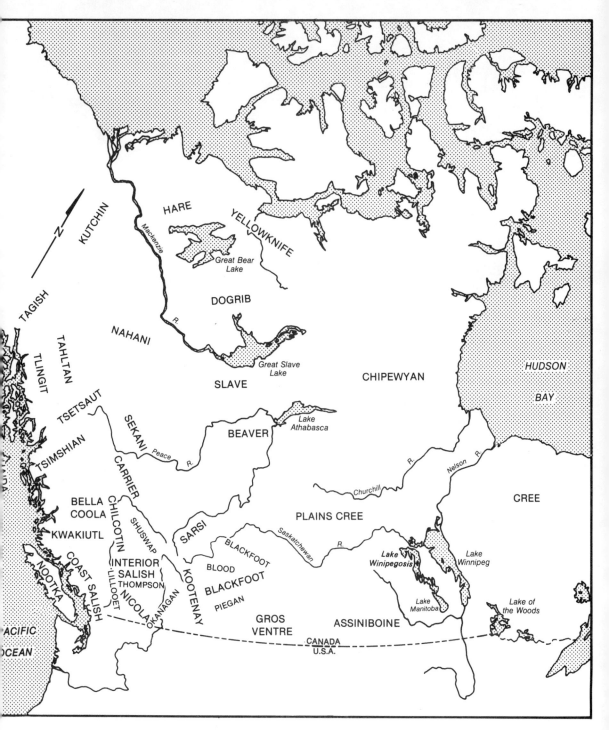

Approximate location of the main tribes of western Canada around 1725.

Métis encampment. The famous Red River carts, used on buffalo hunts and for hauling freight, were light, strong, easily repaired and could serve as rafts for river crossings.

mixed Indian and European origins. They are the product of a particular historical experience. The fur trade competition of the late eighteenth and early nineteenth centuries brought increasing numbers of Europeans to the West. Along the trade routes and at trading posts, marriage and informal ties between Indian women and non-Indian men led to an increase in the number of persons of mixed race. The two tribes most deeply involved in the fur trade at this time were the Ojibwa of the Upper Great Lakes and westward and the Cree who lived in the areas drained by rivers which flow into Hudson Bay. The Indian parentage of the Métis is therefore mainly Cree and Ojibwa. The European parentage was predominantly French Canadian and Scottish with English and English Canadian forming other elements.

Rivalry for the Fur Trade and the Origins of the Métis
Two companies dominated the fur trade, the Hudson's Bay Company and the North West Company. Employees of the former were largely Lowland Scots and Orkney Islanders. The North

West Company was ethnically divided: the higher jobs were held by Highland Scots and Canadians, often of Highland origins; the labouring jobs most often were taken by French Canadians. Highlanders and French Canadians had marriage and religious ties to each other. The Hudson's Bay Company attempted to regulate its employees and their families, while the North West Company was more informal and exercised less control over its employees. Mixed offspring came from all of these men, but the children of Hudson's Bay Company employees were likely to have the advantage of efforts to fit them into company service and the chance to rise within it. Non-English speaking employees of the North West Company were less likely to move up in that company.

In 1821 the two companies united, keeping the name Hudson's Bay Company. Many employees were obliged to retire. The colony at Red River in Manitoba developed as a community for those among these people who did not wish to go east or to Scotland or England. Many of them were of mixed race. The community was controlled by the Hudson's Bay Company and was socially divided according to rank in the company or family ties to the company. English-speaking people dominated, and to be of Scots-Indian or English-Indian descent offered more social and employment opportunities than to be of French-Indian descent. Traders in the company, which was also the government, sought to give educational, job and marriage opportunities to their children.

Before 1821 the North West Company had encouraged its employees of mixed race to think of the Red River area as their land and to resist European settlers coming in. Efforts made by Lord Selkirk to settle Scottish and Irish farmers around Red River met armed resistance. Led by Cuthbert Grant, of English-speaking Scots-Cree-French-Canadian family connections, a company of Métis under their own flag attacked Selkirk's settlers at the Battle of Seven Oaks (1816) in the so-called Pemmican War. After the union of the two fur-trading companies, the governor of the Hudson's Bay Company, George Simpson, appointed Grant to a position in the company. Grant later created his own town and was made Warden of the Plains, a kind of overseer of his people and territory for the company.

The main Métis community developed at Red River. About 80 percent of the settlers there were of mixed race, and of those most were French-speaking Roman Catholics. Conflict with the company over trade, government and the administration of the colony as well as rivalry with nearby Sioux Indians helped to develop a sense of separate Métis identity. They called themselves the New Nation and the *Bois Brulés*, that is the "charred-" or "scorched-wood" people. Pierre Falcon, a Métis poet, wrote about their experiences and composed what he intended as a national anthem for the Métis. The 1840s and 1850s produced other leaders and heroes, among them Guillaume Sayer, who defied the Hudson's Bay Company monopoly and insisted on their right to trade furs on their own.

Although the Métis did some farming, this was a difficult and undependable livelihood. The buffalo hunt and fur trading were the basis of their economy and lifestyle. The buffalo hunt was a community affair, organized with a Métis-run government which operated while the hunt was in progress. In order to carry their supplies as they moved about and the meat produced by the hunt, they invented a two-wheeled cart known as the Red River cart. Its huge wooden wheels turning on a wooden axle made a piercing, shrieking noise which could be heard over great distances.

The Métis Buffalo Hunt—Summer 1846

"The [Métis] are a very hardy race of men, capable of enduring the greatest hardships and fatigues ... Their buffalo hunts are conducted by the whole tribe, and take place twice a year, about the middle of June and October, at which periods notice is sent round to all the families to meet at a certain day on the White Horse Plain, about twenty miles [thirty-two kilometres] from Fort Garry. Here the tribe is divided into three bands, each taking a separate route for the purpose of falling in with the herds of buffaloes. These bands are each accompanied by about 500 carts, drawn by either an ox or a horse. Their cart is a curious-looking vehicle, made by themselves with their own axes, and fastened together with wooden pins and leather strings, nails not being procurable. The tire of the wheel is made of buffalo hide, and put on wet; when it becomes dry it shrinks, and is so tight that it never falls off, and lasts as long as the cart holds together."

PAUL KANE
WANDERINGS OF AN ARTIST

The Métis lived far away from any major European settlement. Over the decades from the late eighteenth to the late nineteenth century, this isolation along with their family ties to Indians and to each other gave them a strong sense of community and independence and self-reliance.

When arrangements were made. in the late 1860s for the Hudson's Bay Company to transfer control of Rupert's Land to Canada, the Métis felt that their land and their independence were threatened. They were not consulted and had no part in the transfer. In 1869 they rose in rebellion at Red River Colony in an effort to control their future. Their leader was Louis Riel, an educated and able young man whose family had been active in the colony's public affairs. They called for provincial status and representation in Ottawa as well as recognition of their ownership of their farms. To some degree they were successful: the area around the colony entered Confederation as the Province of Manitoba in 1870. Nevertheless, changes in land title and ways of dividing up the land made them unhappy and fearful. As settlers began coming into the new province the Métis found themselves outnumbered. Although their land was assured them or they were given payment for it, many chose to move farther west.

In the mid-1880s the Métis were again threatened and again they resisted with force. Riel, who was living in exile in Montana, was asked to lead again and came into Saskatchewan to take charge. This second rising was quickly crushed and Riel was executed for treason. Only in recent decades have the Métis begun to reassert themselves as a separate people, a people of mixed race, of French language, but without legal Indian status.

Phase III: Losing Freedom—From Voluntary to Involuntary Change

The experience of contact with the Europeans was unique for each group, band or tribe. Nevertheless, over a period of several hundred years in the case of the eastern Indians and over a much shorter time in that of western and northern Indians, contact with the newcomers helped to change all of the different peoples who were called Indians. To that extent, contact with the Europeans provided common experiences that all Indians shared.

Partners and Employees

The Indians, as we have seen, became partners and employees in the fur trade industry. They took advantage of the trade goods they received in exchange for fur pelts—guns, iron tools, metal kettles and knives, cloth and other items—to improve their standard of living. A Micmac chief spoke of the beaver as "making" all kinds of things because it could be traded for a variety of items which gradually took the place of traditional ones. As Indians came to rely on the new, they stopped making their own objects. They became dependent on the fur trade and employment in it for the things they needed and wished to have but which they could not make. The early voluntary ties to the European economy and technology became more difficult to break.

Tribes shifted to new locations in order to get pelts. They invaded each other's territory, travelled far from home, took orders from the European and turned to new occupations. Tribes traditionally located along the coast moved inland to trap; tribes of the woodlands moved into the plains to hunt. Hunters began to have vegetable plots in order to sell their produce to trading posts. Individuals became canoemen, carriers, guides, and inter-

The tipi of the Plains Indians was covered with buffalo skins and was similar in shape and structure to the wigwams of the woodland Indians. Instead of a simple smoke-hole at the top, however, it had flaps, or "ears," that could be moved by means of poles according to the direction of the wind. Not all tipis were painted like the one in this picture. The design of those which were came to the owners as a vision and had deep spiritual significance. This tipi belonged to a Blood medicine man. Note the medicine bundle suspended near the entrance.

preters. Some acted as middlemen, trading with more remote Indians and delivering the pelts to the forts. Women who had prepared dried meat for their families began to make pemmican to sell to traders. Other women married non-Indians and sometimes found themselves learning many new ways to live. A successful hunter might be made "chief" by the trading company.

The changes brought about by contact with the Europeans thus affected not only the Indians' way of making a living and their technology, but also their place of residence and their political organization. The balance between humans and their food resources had often been delicate in pre-European days when people were hunting, fishing and gathering only what they needed in order to live. The introduction of commercial hunting and trapping proved too much for the wildlife in some areas. Not only did this force people to move, it also resulted in friction with others and increased dependence on the trading posts. Sometimes peoples had to split up into smaller units in order to survive.

Competition for territory and trade led to new kinds of war. To the traditional raiding and feuding for revenge, prestige, kidnapping and horse-capturing was added warfare on a larger and deadlier scale. Tribes and bands pressed to have uncontested access to trade items, including guns and ammunition. Traditional rivalries were exaggerated and tribes were drawn into competition. The Blackfoot-Cree rivalry of the nineteenth century was an example of such a change. To defend themselves tribes drew together into alliances, confederacies and leagues; the Council of Three Fires and the Blackfoot Confederacy mentioned earlier may serve as examples.

Population: Decline and Movement

The population of many Indian tribes declined significantly after the arrival of the Europeans. The major cause was epidemic diseases introduced by the Europeans—smallpox, measles, diptheria, influenza, scarlet fever, tuberculosis and others. Europeans had developed a certain degree of immunity to these diseases, but the Indians, who had none, died by the thousands. Tribes and bands were reduced time after time as epidemics swept through them.

Regroupings of peoples occurred as a result of population decline, food decline, shifts to new areas and the new dependent condition. Some experts believe that food shortages contributed to the spread of the idea of a supernatural cannibal spirit (Windigo) which drove people mad. Social and religious ceremonies developed which gave strength and unity to the new groupings, forming and re-forming.

Population movement led to greater contact among peoples and resulted in more cultural borrowing not only from the Europeans but from other Indians. Cree Indians spread from Hudson Bay to the Rocky Mountains. Iroquois employees in the fur trade travelled to Alberta. In the early and mid-eighteenth century Ojibwa moved southeast into southern Ontario. There they clashed with the Iroquois who had been using the area as hunting territory since the dispersal of the Hurons, Tobacco and Neutrals. Tradition says the Ojibwa and Iroquois fought several battles, then they resolved their differences, and the Ojibwa took up permanent residence in much of southern Ontario.

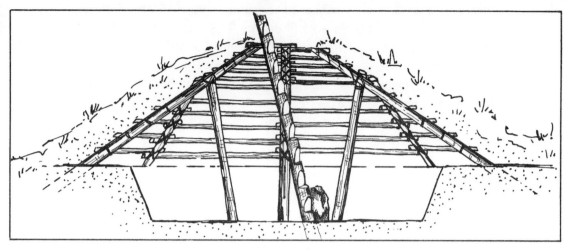

The Interior Salish people built winter houses that were partly underground. About nine metres in diameter, the houses were circular and were entered by a ladder from the roof. They were covered over with earth and were quite warm, though often water seeped in.

Abenaki Indians immigrated into Quebec from New England in the seventeenth century. In the late eighteenth century Iroquois and Delaware immigrated into southern Ontario, and in the early nineteenth century Potawatomi also entered Ontario.

The boundaries of the Chipewyan and Cree shifted north and south in the eighteenth century, and the Blackfoot, as we have seen, moved westward from central Saskatchewan into southern Alberta after about 1750. About the same time a branch of the Athapascan-speaking Beaver Indians, the Sarsi, moved southward and became allies of the three Blackfoot groups.

Survival with Change

Despite these changes, or because of them in some cases, the cultures of most of the Indians remained intact. There had been changes during the centuries before the Europeans came, and the Indians' flexibility and adaptability made it possible for them to hold onto their traditions while adjusting and moulding them to changed conditions.

Ottawa Indians took up the Huron Feast of the Dead ceremonies. The Huron periodically exhumed, cleaned and re-buried the bones of all of those who had died since the last Feast of the Dead. This custom is thought to have helped to emphasize their common identity and sense of community, and the Ottawa adopted it as an aid to social unity. The Blackfoot acquired "medicine bundles," religious and ceremonial objects, from the Upper Missouri River peoples. At first they bought actual bundles and then began to create their own. The contents were associated with supernatural experiences and were religious heirlooms as well as items connected with the new wealth of the "golden age" of Plains Indians.

Indian religious leaders offered interpretations of religion and philosophy. Sometimes seen as prophets or messiahs, they proposed rejection or selective acceptance of European culture. On a few occasions military movements developed from the religious message. The Pontiac uprising, for example, was inspired to a great extent by the ideas of a religious leader known as the Delaware Prophet.

The Longhouse Religion among the Six Nations Iroquois spread into Canada from New York. In the early nineteenth cen-

Masks representing evil spirits, used in the healing rituals of the Iroquois False Face Society.

tury, the Seneca prophet Handsome Lake revived the traditional Iroquois religion, emphasizing moral and spirital values as well as healing ceremonies. This religion continued to grow and vigourously expand into the late twentieth century.

The late eighteenth and early nineteenth centuries introduced an important new factor that Indians would have to deal with: a great increase in the number of settlers. Throughout the previous centuries the number of Europeans had been small. Fewer than one hundred thousand French settlers were in Canada by the last quarter of the eighteenth century. As for the fur traders, their business required them to employ Indians in all aspects of the trade, and they had no intention of destroying the source of their fur supply. There was apparently no long range planning beyond getting pelts, yet the influences for change which were introduced were considerable. The effects spread from tribe to tribe and also from some aspects of tribal life to others—from ways of making a living and making what was needed, to where one lived, to who governed and how, to one's religion and values. All of this, however, had so far occurred in conditions where the Indians were important to the total economy and had many personal ties to the Europeans. A very different situation was developing in eastern and central Canada in the late 1700s and early 1800s as a large number of immigrants came from Britain and the United States.

In the light of what came later, the days of the fur trade were looked back to as in some ways a golden age, an age of the flowering of Indian cultures. It was a period of rising standard of living and material improvements; the horse and gun, metal tools and utensils, new foods and clothes made life easier, but the old customs and beliefs remained basically intact.

Phase IV: "Strangers in Our Own Land"—Forced Change

From their earliest contact with Europeans, Indians had borrowed and exchanged goods and services. As their desire for European products grew and extended to more and more goods and trade items, their dependency increased. A kind of easing of this dependency was possible if there was more than one trading partner. Competition among various groups of Europeans increased the supply of trade goods and lowered the price; but it also brought conflict and even violence. More time had to be given to hunting and trapping for commercial purposes, and less was available for activities directly related to subsistence. Old skills in making things for use were abandoned, if not forgotten.

In many cases leaders were appointed by the Europeans instead of being chosen by the Indians themselves. Where dealing with the Europeans was important for survival, this had to be tolerated even if it was not welcomed. There was a gradual shift from a position in which change was voluntary to one in which changes were a necessity, a condition of getting trade goods and selling products—furs, fish, meat, services—to a fur company.

When the numbers of Europeans began to increase rapidly and larger areas of land were required for farming, mining, logging, towns, roads and other uses, the Indians experienced a new loss of control of their own lives.

The Reserves

In the late eighteenth century immigrants from Europe and the United States came to the Maritime Provinces, the southern portion of central Canada, Ontario and Quebec. These people wanted to develop the forms of government they were accus-

The Indians believed that sickness was caused by an evil spirit which had to be cast out or appeased. The person who could do this was the medicine man or shaman, who had acquired special powers through prayer and fasting. Here a Tsimshian medicine man at Kitwanga, B.C. has been called upon to cure an ailing child. Drum-beating, singing and the shaking of rattles were all part of the curing ritual.

tomed to and use the land in ways that were familiar to them. This meant controlling the native people and their land. The fur trade would no longer be the basis of the economy. Fur trading continued but became less important generally and especially in the areas of major settlement.

The Indians' place in this new economy was not nearly as important as it had been in the fur trade. Most were unfamiliar with farming. Disease and other causes had greatly reduced their numbers, and large new immigrant populations were coming in. To clear the land for these new arrivals, the natives were placed upon reserves. These were located within the areas the tribes had long occupied, but were greatly reduced in size from the territory they had previously had for their own. In the Maritimes and Quebec these reserves were created as the need arose. In Ontario treaties were signed with the Indians occupying an area the government wanted. By the late eighteenth and early nineteenth century most of southern Ontario had passed into the hands of the Ojibwa, and so it was with these people that the treaties surrendering land were made. From the area surrendered, small portions were set aside as the homeland of the natives. These were reserves.

The government and the people involved in creating these new circumstances were not completely indifferent to the way changes were affecting the Indians. Some tried to find an organized and consistent way of introducing them to life as settled farmers, trained in European civilization and with European ways and beliefs.

In the nineteenth century both Indians and non-Indians noticed the decline in Indian population. Many thought Indians would die out altogether. Others believed that the only chance for them as a people was to give up most or all of their old ways—their religion, language, economy, housing, clothes, marriage customs, social and political customs and so forth. This could best be accomplished, it was felt, by putting them under non-native government control. With the help of missionaries, teachers and businesses, government officials took charge of their lives in order to bring about the desired changes. Change, once voluntary, was now being forced upon the Indians. They would no longer be free to direct their own lives, either public or personal.

The reserve was thus meant to serve two major purposes at once: to release larger land areas from Indian control and to provide a place of regulated settlement where Indians could be made over into Europeanized people. "Protection and advancement" was the slogan of the government's Indian administration.

The Treaties

The idea of selling land was generally unknown to the Indians, and this meant that the treaty surrenders were usually based on misunderstanding. Among most native communities the political and social leaders had no authority to sell land on behalf of the whole group. In fact, no one in the native community had such power or authority.

The Indians' view of the land was that it was alive. They sometimes referred to it as their "mother," feeding and sheltering them and keeping them alive. When they signed treaties they

"Our land is more valuable than your money. It will last forever. It will not perish as long as the sun shines and the water flows, and through all the years it will give life to men and beasts."

"We cannot sell the lives of men and animals, and therefore we cannot sell the land. It was put here by the Great Spirit and we cannot sell it because it does not really belong to us. You can count your money and burn it with the nod of a buffalo's head, but only the Great Spirit can count the grains of sand and the blades of grass on these plains. As a present to you we will give you anything we have that you can take with you, the land we cannot give."

CROWFOOT

thought they were sharing this with others, allowing the new-comers to make use of the resources which they also used. The treaties were regarded as agreements to trade and to live in friend-ship and peace.

Often it was not until some time later that the Indians discovered this was an incomplete if not entirely mistaken view of what they had agreed to. The signing of the treaties usually included much speech making and perhaps verbal promises. Among the Indians most knowledge and information was passed by word of mouth. To them what was said was as binding as what was written down. This too proved to be a mistaken idea. Treaties were business contracts with little or none of the poetic language of "rivers running," "grass growing" and "sun rising and setting."

The tradition of treaties of land surrender dates at least from the middle 1700s when the government in London decided that it alone had the right to purchase land from the Indians. Private persons and local governments were forbidden to do so. In exchange for land surrender the Indians were paid in goods and supplies such as cloth, ammunition and metal tools. Later a yearly payment was made in goods and money or in money only, at the government's discretion.

In 1850, under the two Robinson treaties (named after the government negotiator), the Ojibwa gave up their land north of Lake Superior and Lake Huron. These treaties became models for the later so-called "numbered treaties." Their terms included the location of the reserve to be created; the granting of annual payments of money (annuities) to each member of the band sign-

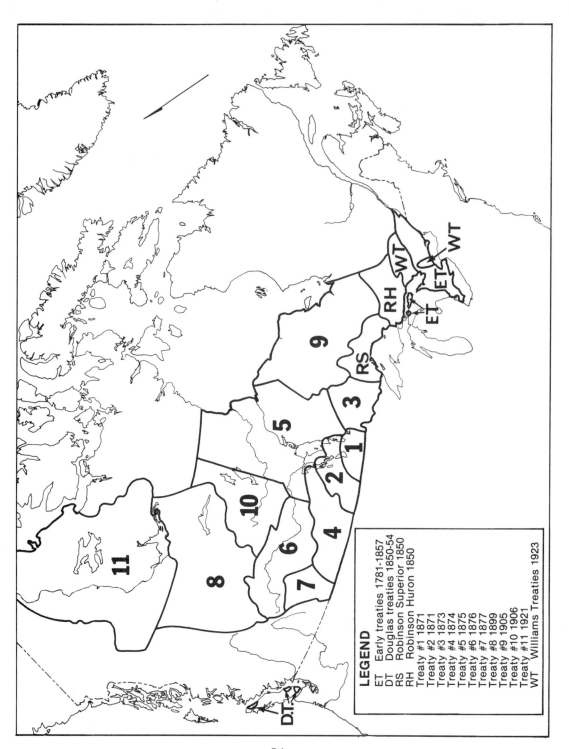

LEGEND

ET Early treaties 1781-1857
DT Douglas treaties 1850-54
RS Robinson Superior 1850
RH Robinson Huron 1850

Treaty #1 1871
Treaty #2 1871
Treaty #3 1873
Treaty #4 1874
Treaty #5 1875
Treaty #6 1876
Treaty #7 1877
Treaty #8 1899
Treaty #9 1905
Treaty #10 1906
Treaty #11 1921
WT Williams Treaties 1923

ing the treaty, with larger payments to chiefs and leaders; and the granting of freedom to hunt and fish in the surrendered area until it was taken up by non-Indians.

More treaties were signed as plans were made for settlers to move westward. In 1870, when Canada got possession of the former Hudson's Bay Company territory of Rupert's Land, only a small part of it became the province of Manitoba. Most of it, including the future provinces of Alberta and Saskatchewan, became the Northwest Territories. To prepare for the settlers, a series of treaties were signed with the Indians in the southern portions of these areas between 1871 and 1877. These treaties were numbered from one to seven and are known as the "numbered treaties." (Four more treaties, numbered eight to eleven, were signed later, between 1899 and 1921.)

In 1871 Sweetgrass, a Cree Chief, told the government of the dangers to Indians because of loss of game and fear of loss of game. He asked for technical aid and other forms of assistance which would enable the Indians to adapt to the new situation.

Treaty Number One (1871) was signed at Fort Garry. The speeches that went on for eight days before the signing showed that the Indians did not clearly grasp what was happening. They asked for a reserve which would have included two-thirds of what was then a much smaller Province of Manitoba. Instead they were to be granted 160 acres (about 65 hectares) for a family of five, an annual payment of three dollars per person in cash or goods (the government to decide), and a school on the reserve. All the other treaties were modelled on this one, though some changes were made. The amount of land per family of five was raised to 640 acres (about 260 hectares) in Treaty Number Three, and the payments were increased to five dollars per year. Chiefs and headmen were given more money than others and a uniform every three years.

In Treaty Number Six, chiefs got a horse, wagon and harness in addition to other payments. Even so, Big Bear, a Plains Cree chief, refused for several years to accept the terms and change his way of life. Other Cree who thought as he did joined him. Sweet-

Map showing the areas of land surrendered by treaty.

grass, Starblanket and Big Child signed. Lucky Man and Little Pine held out for a short time and then signed. Treaty Number Seven was signed at Blackfoot Crossing by Crowfoot, Old Sun, Red Crow, Heavy Shield and Rainy Chief for the Blackfoot. Bull Head signed for the Sarsi.

Missionaries, the North West Mounted Police and Hudson's Bay Company employees had encouraged the Indians to sign the treaties. They had explained their meaning, but since the concept of a treaty was unknown to the Indians and since the powers of the chief were limited, misunderstanding was certain. Friendship, sharing, cooperation and assistance may have been the understanding of the Indians.

Confinement to reserves did not begin at once for the signers of Treaties One to Seven. Those Indians who made their living by hunting the buffalo were able to continue in their old ways for a time. It was several years before the buffalo declined almost to the point of vanishing and about ten years until the completion of the railway speeded up the flow of settlers. By the early 1880s, however, reserves had been surveyed and pressure was being put on the Indians to take up the new way of life.

Important in this new way was farming. In order to farm, instruction, equipment, livestock and good weather were minimum requirements. All of these were in inadequate supply or entirely lacking. The early 1880s saw drought or near drought in parts of the Prairies. The nation was in an economic low period. Qualified and conscientious people willing to act as advisers to the Indians were few.

For people who had never farmed or gardened, it was a very bad time to have to begin.

Resistance

Dissatisfaction arose as Indians turned to their new controllers, the Indian Administration officers, for food and aid. When they were left waiting or received little help, resentment grew. Some felt desperate and resorted to desperate measures. In the summer, of 1884, Chief Yellow Calf and members of his band broke into a warehouse to get needed supplies. About the same time, Métis leaders invited Cree, Assiniboine and Blackfoot to join them in rebellion against the starvation conditions which threatened their

Louis Riel, leader of the 1869-70 uprising at Red River and the Northwest Rebellions of 1885.

existence. Plains Cree chiefs Poundmaker and Big Bear joined, but they did so reluctantly and their part in the fighting was small. Most of the people did not rise. Blackfoot chief Crowfoot, like Cree chiefs Starblanket and Big Child, rejected the invitation.

After the Riel uprising was crushed, Poundmaker and Big Bear were imprisoned. Both died not long after their release from confinement.

The Dene and British Columbia

Treaties were later signed with the Dene Indians covering the western portion of today's Northwest Territories and a small portion of the Yukon Territory. Once again these treaties were part of planned expansion into the area. The Dene Indians, like most others before them, have continued to understand the agreements they signed differently than the government.

In British Columbia, only a very little land was surrendered by treaty. In the early 1850s Governor James Douglas concluded fourteen treaties with Indians at Victoria, Nanaimo and Fort Rupert on Vancouver Island. The Indians at these places surrendered their land forever in exchange for a small payment per family and reserves composed of their villages and nearby fields. They were allowed to hunt and fish in the surrendered area as long as it was not occupied by non-Indians. The northeast corner of British Columbia was also surrendered by treaty in 1899 (Treaty Number Eight). But for the most part, the Indians' land was simply taken over without treaties and without adequate consultation and compensation.

In the 1880s the Indians protested. They objected to reserves being assigned them as inadequate and unjust. Some non-Indians feared that the British Columbia tribes would rebel as some Plains Indians were doing at the time. The authorities were so worried that a small expedition of troops was sent to the Skeena River when a local murder was reported in Victoria as an uprising by Tsimshian Indians. The Tsimshian have had a long history of protest over land claims.

The Indian Act

The Maritime Provinces, Quebec, most of the Yukon Territory and most of British Columbia were not subject to land surrender treaties. Nevertheless, with the exception of the Dene and others in the two northern territories, most Indians in these areas too were enrolled in registered Indian communities, or bands, and reserves, one or more, were assigned to each band. This development was made possible by a law of 1876, the Indian Act.

The British North America Act of 1867 had made the federal government responsible for Indians and Indian land. The government later passed the Indian Act in order to have one overriding law to govern and train the Indians and one centrally controlled administration to deal with them. This gave a similarity of purpose and technique to the management of Indian affairs throughout the country.

The policy behind the Indian Act was a continuation of the policy of "protection and advancement" that had begun to develop in the 1820s and 1830s in eastern Canada. The Indians, having surrendered the greater part of their land, were to be placed in controlled communities where they could undergo the changes already referred to, that is, a complete change of culture. Individuals and bands would be trained to cease to be Indians. Full citizenship in Canada would then be available to them.

Indian Status

The Indian Act created the legal, or status, Indian. Under its terms, only a person who was legally enrolled as an Indian and in a particular band was an Indian. Children and later generations had to be descended on the father's side of the family from someone who was an Indian in the eyes of the law. "Status" or "registered" or, in the Prairie Provinces, "treaty Indian" are the terms used. Only those who were Indians under the terms of the Indian Act could live on reserves, participate in any treaty or other benefits, receive assistance from the Department of Indian Affairs and be a regular part of their Indian community. Legal means were created for a person to surrender Indian status, and a provision was included under which Indian women marrying non-Indians would automatically lose their legal Indian status. The Indian Act, though modified, has remained in force into the 1980s.

Effects on the Indians

By the time the Indian Act was passed, the Indians had undergone many changes. But their values and ideals had changed little or not at all. Family and kinship, social and religious institutions were largely still alive and working. The Indians were still attempting to adapt and modify; now they were being told to make themselves into something else. They could not and would not do this, and the federal administration placed over them had neither the knowledge nor the skill, the staff nor the power to stamp out their culture. The efforts of the government, schools, churches and businesses were only partially successful.

In the late nineteenth century, as we have seen, some Indian customs were made illegal. Other forced changes later resulted from an amendment to the Indian Act which introduced parliamentary forms to band governments. This amendment provided for Canadian-style elections, representation, and terms of office, with elected chiefs and band councillors. Unfortunately, the effort to have the Indians take up parliamentary democracy was made meaningless by the fact that a government official, the Indian Superintendent, or Indian Agent, had the power to override the elected councils and control Indian community matters.

Indians were the only people in Canada who had a federal department controlling them (the department was moved from ministry to ministry from the 1870s to the 1980s). As their numbers declined both absolutely and relatively during the late nineteenth and early twentieth century, they were without power.

Many Indians began to take unskilled or semi-skilled jobs off the reserves in agriculture, mining, logging, ranching, fishing and other rural occupations. In northern areas hunting and trapping continued to be important sources of work. Whether on or off the reserves, the main type of employment was seasonal, outdoor, physical labour. As working for wages replaced the Indians' efforts to farm, farms declined and Indian land was leased to non-Indian farmers and ranchers. Problems of protecting the reserves from poachers weakened efforts to have reserve logging industries. Government regulations which prevented taking loans on reserve property also blocked development and therefore the creation of jobs. Handicraft products could not compete with machine-produced goods. Racial discrimination became a regular

One of the terms of the treaties of land surrender was an annual cash payment which came to be known as "treaty money." Government agents are seen here paying out treaty money to Manitoba Indians in 1880.

feature of Indian experience, especially near reserves. All around the native peoples, the newcomers dominated.

Indians and Missionaries

As we have seen, a strong emphasis on spiritual support for everyday life was a trait of the Indians. To be good at one's job, whether it was hunting, making canoes, curing the sick or some other task, required spiritual help.

When Christian missionaries arrived to teach and convert the Indians, they were seen as people who had contact with the supernatural and who therefore had or might have the kind of power which could be used by the Indian. The missionaries had tools and goods which the Indians desired. They also had religious and ceremonial objects—crosses, Bibles, prayer beads, writing—which seemed to give them power.

During the period when voluntary change was taking place and a kind of partnership existed between Indians and Europeans, missionaries were received as another new element which might improve life for the people. They visited the Indians or lived with them, evangelizing them and training converts to spread the gospels. Sometimes they established a mission station where they resided for a portion of the year. It became the home base from which they travelled to surrounding areas. They might cover thousands of kilometres every year, suffering the hardships of winter and summer, forests and prairies, by foot, horseback, canoe and cart, to teach, preach, heal, advise and perform other services.

One of the remarkable types of missions established was the Christian Village. Both Protestant and Roman Catholic missionaries used this technique. The earliest, Sillery, was founded in Quebec in 1637, and the practice was still used in the late nineteenth century in British Columbia. The most famous of these later Christian Villages was Metlakatla, near Prince George, British Columbia, founded by William Duncan in 1862.

The Christian Village was composed of converts and possible converts who lived under the religious, political and economic control of the missionary. People came voluntarily, but to stay they had to accept the authority of the missionary. Perhaps the Indians who came to live in these villages for shorter or longer

61

A Description of a Church Service at Metlakatla, B.C. in 1867
"It was a pretty sight to see the whole population, old and young, at the sound of the bell, thronging to worship God. No need to lock doors, for there is no one to enter the empty houses. Every soul is assembled in the one place, and for one purpose. As they entered, the men took the right and the women the left hand of the great circular hall. . . . Service began with a hymn in Tsimshian. [William Duncan] led with his concertina. The air was very plaintive and beautiful—sung by some 200 voices, men, women, and children. . . Then followed prayers in Tsimshian, at the close of which all joined in the Lord's Prayer in English. Then followed a chant; one of the Psalms he had translated and taught them, to a fine old Gregorian. His address, or sermon, of nearly an hour, was upon the story of Martha and Mary. His manner and gesticulation were animated and striking, very much after their own style. Their attention never seemed to flag throughout."

HENRY S. WELLCOME
THE STORY OF METLAKAHTLA (1887)

periods of time found that the advantages of protection, work, security and assistance balanced the disadvantages of missionary control. When Indians passed under federal Indian administration, many of the tasks which the missionaries had performed were taken over by the government.

Generally speaking, the Indians were tolerant of the new religious teachers and saw them as useful allies in their efforts to adapt to the changes being introduced. This willingness to combine their ways with the new ones often meant that Indians did not change as much or as rapidly as the missionaries wished them to. By the nineteenth century, the missionaries were insisting that becoming a Christian meant abandoning many Indian ways and adopting a European way of life. It might mean giving up traditional clothes, housing, oocupations, education, religion, ceremonies, social and marriage customs, names and attitudes. The old life was seldom seen as capable of being developed into something new and good. It was not to be built onto, but to be destroyed. Life on the reserve or in the Christian Village was supposed to bring this about. Native culture was looked down on and often described in abusive terms. The people were seen as backward or childlike and to be drastically changed.

Of the three major denominations working among the Indians, the first were the Roman Catholics. The Jesuits and later

Father Albert Lacombe (1827-1916), seen here with Crowfoot (centre) and other chiefs, was one of the first Roman Catholic missionaries in the Northwest. He founded churches and schools, helped the Indians adjust to an agricultural way of life and was several times instrumental in preventing bloodshed.

the Oblates of Mary Immaculate were the two most prominent missionary societies of the Roman Catholic Church, though other groups such as the Franciscans and Sulpicians were also active. The Recollets, a sub-order of Franciscans, and the Jesuits pioneered Christian missions in eastern and central Canada in the early seventeenth century. Some of the most famous Jesuit missionaries worked among the Hurons and were responsible for converting some of them and for their links to the French fur trade. Several were killed in the war between the Huron and Iroquois.

The two major Protestant denominations were the Anglicans and the Methodists. (The Methodists later joined other denominations to form the United Church of Canada.) The Anglicans were active among the Iroquois Indians before some of them migrated to Canada after the American Revolution; Joseph Brant was an Anglican. The main mission work, however, was carried out by a group formed in England in 1799, the Church Missionary Society, which came to Canada in the 1820s.

The Methodist missions began in the early nineteenth century, and they are notable for the number of Indian clergymen they quickly produced among the Ontario Ojibwa. Especially famous as a Methodist preacher and Indian public figure was the Mississauga-Welsh Peter Jones. One Ojibwa Methodist clergyman, Henry Bird Steinhauer (he took the name of his adoptive parents), became a missionary to the Cree Indians of western Canada. His descendant Ralph Steinhauer became lieutenant-governor of Alberta in the 1970s.

Missions and missionaries were especially active in educating the Indians, and until the second half of the twentieth century most Indians would have received their formal education from mission schools. In a variety of ways the missionaries were, throughout their history, informally and formally part of the impact of European civilization.

Phase V: Rebirth of the People

The second half of the twentieth century has seen native peoples in various parts of the world, but especially in Asia and Africa, regain control of their lands, their government and their culture from the countries which had conquered them. A form of this process has taken place among the Indian people of Canada.

Indians and non-Indians, looking at population trends in the late nineteenth century, predicted that Indians would disappear as a separate racial and cultural group or groups. Epidemic diseases had reduced the population. Intermarriage and intermixing were taking place. Discrimination and prejudice against Indians caused some of them to deny their Indian backgrounds, and many tried to take up the new road of the Canadian newcomers. The schools and reserves, as we have seen, were meant to be training grounds where Indians would lose their old culture.

Population Rise and Indian Organizations

By the early 1900s, however, careful observers had begun to notice two unexpected trends. Most Canadians remained unaware of these trends until the mid-twentieth century. First, the Indian population (that is, the number of Indians under the law, status Indians, or as they are called in several provinces, treaty Indians) was rising. Non-status Indians and Métis were increasing in numbers as well. Census figures began to show an upturn in total numbers of Indians early in the century, but it was not until later that parallel growth could be seen among the Métis. For many decades after the defeat and humiliation of the 1885 rebellion, Métis people had denied their background, but a new sense of identity began to be seen among them around mid-century.

Blood medicine woman.

Secondly, along with the upturn in population, the period after World War I saw an increasing number of Indian organizations, Indian leaders, protest movements and lobbying with government.

The various tribes had all undergone changes over the years. But after several decades or more of federal government administration they had also come to share similar experiences. Schools brought together young people from different reserves and tribes. Native organizations and native social events, such as powwows and seasonal festivals, including the Calgary Stampede, caused people to meet and exchange ideas and information. Transportation and communication improved opportunities for contact, and the widespread use of the English language aided in the creation of an all-Indian, or Pan-Indian, identity.

Tourists, entertainment and business interests gave an additional boost to this trend through movies and the sale of "Indian" souvenirs. Birchbark canoes, tipis, feather bonnets, totem poles, moccassins and other artifacts came to be seen as part of the Indian way of life, even though these articles were not found among all Indians. Indians have had to struggle to change the non-Indians' view of them, which was distorted by this oversimplified picture.

The chiefs of the traditional culture had been transformed into elected chiefs and councillors of the Indian band. Though they had little power under the Indian Agents, they and other leaders, such as elders and wise old people, who were not in government-sanctioned positions provided continuity with the past. It is noticeable even in the late twentieth century that the leadership at band level and at tribal, provincial and national levels is often held by men and women whose families have long served in that role.

The Grand General Indian Council
The history of the Indians reveals the existence of numerous intertribal organizations over the past several hundred years. The Confederacy of the Iroquois (six nations after the Tuscarora joined) and the Council of Three Fires are only two examples. The Grand General Indian Council was formed in Ontario in the 1850s. It was made up mainly of Ojibwa, but soon came to include Quebec and Maritime Indians. The organization issued statements which told of their members' interests and concerns. At a conference held in 1894, the Council called for revisions to the Indian Act. Specific articles in the Act were mentioned, aid to the poor was requested, and forced enfranchisement was opposed on the grounds that the Indians were not yet ready. Some of those attending the conference wanted to suppress the use of alcohol, while others urged that Indians should have equality with non-Indians in its use. Band membership was also discussed. Who should be admitted? Who should get the yearly payments and annuities? The 1894 conference also noted that the federal Indian administration ignored Indian opinion and asked for Indian control of reserve resources. Most of these issues, perhaps in different forms, have continued to be of concern to Indians.

Other Indian organizations came into existence in the early twentieth century. They reflected the growing number of Indians who were becoming skilful in working through European-style, voluntary, interest-group associations.

The Allied Tribes of British Columbia
The Allied Tribes of British Columbia was formed in 1915. It represented especially the coastal tribes, and its main objective

was to bring their loss of land and the lack of land treaties in British Columbia to the attention of provincial and federal authorities. It had not achieved its goals by the time it broke up in 1927 when its demands were refused and its protest forbidden, but many of its members continued to be active in later British Columbia Indian organizations. Two of its leaders, Andrew Paull (Squamish) and Peter Kelly (Haida), became leaders in the Native Brotherhood of British Columbia, which was formed in 1931. This organization is still active. It has been important in urging that native culture be encouraged to grow and expand within the modern life of the coastal fishing peoples. In the 1920s the League of Indians of Canada was formed, and Edward Ahena-kew (Plains Cree) became prominent in that organization.

The North American Indian Brotherhood

In 1944 Andrew Paull founded the North American Indian Brotherhood (NAIB), which was intended to be a national and even international organization. Paull's career greatly influenced that of George Manuel, who was responsible for calling the first international conference of Indians from North and South America.

The main aim of the NAIB was to unify Indians nationally. Selections from the Preamble to the Constitution of the North American Indian Brotherhood illustrate its intention: "It [the NAIB] aims to salvage material from the ashes of the past, and thereby awaken in the Indian race the dormant nobility which is, by heritage, rightfully theirs. . . ." It "will seek to restore treaty obligations," and "will press for amendments or revisions" of the Indian Act for the well-being of Indians.

The National Indian Brotherhood

The National Indian Brotherhood, founded in 1968, has gone a long way to achieve the unity intended by its forerunner, the NAIB. The White Paper of 1969 made Indians aware that the government was considering drastic changes which would do away with legal protection that the Indian Act and Indian status gave them. After 1969 the various Indian organizations which had come into existence acted more aggressively to protect them-selves. By the 1970s every province and territory in which Indians

On June 4, 1970 two hundred Indians from across Canada gathered in Ottawa to present their answer to the government's White Paper of 1969. Their "Red Paper" totally rejected the government's new policy.

were resident had one or more Indian organizations representing them. One of the main aims of all these groups is given in the aims of the National Indian Brotherhood: "The National Indian Brotherhood will endeavour to secure the enforcement and fulfillment of all Indian treaties and aboriginal rights of Indians."

Rebirth

Harold Cardinal, Cree author and activist, has called the spirit being shown by Indians a rebirth. The development of a greater awareness of the many peoples who have come to make up Canada, their many origins and national and cultural backgrounds has helped to stimulate a greater interest in the history of the Indians. With the study of Indian history has come greater awareness of earlier efforts to stamp out and change their culture.

A combination of Indian and non-Indian interest and awareness has helped create a new condition in which Indians are attempting to play a larger role in shaping their own lives as Indians and as members of Indian communities.

These organizations hope to strengthen the Indians' ability to hold on to what is best from the past, including particular tribal heritages, and enable them to build onto it in the future as Indians and as Canadians. More and more they compare themselves to peoples in Africa and Asia who were conquered by the Europeans at various times since about 1500 and who are now trying to be free to control their lives in all important aspects—political, religious, economic, social.

In the provinces and territories Métis and non-status-Indian organizations have also been formed. At the national level, paralleling the National Indian Brotherhood, is the Native Council of Canada, which speaks for Métis and non-status Indians on a nation-wide basis.

The Fourth World

The African and Asian countries have been called the "Third World." George Manuel has called the Indians of North and South America and others in a similar situation the "Fourth World" to show their still conquered status as minority original peoples.

In the past it was thought that for the Indians being "modern" would mean giving up all that was part of their past. "Civilized" was a word often used to describe the non-Indian newcomers. Indians would be "civilized" if they became like the invaders. "Modern" and "civilized" have lost some of their meaning as both Indians and non-Indians have come to see much good in the thoughts and customs of a variety of peoples. Indian culture has much to offer Indians still, they believe, and some assert that it has traits to offer non-Indians as well. The Indians need not dress in moccasins and feather bonnet, use a canoe or live in a tipi to remember, cherish and preserve elements of their past of their own choosing. As Indians migrate to cities and urban areas they are seeking means to preserve elements of their culture in the new environment. Just as Scottish, Greek, Italian or Pakistani traditions can be adapted to late twentieth-century urban Canadian life without loss of links to the near or distant past, so too Indians expect that this should be possible for them. The Indian may in this way be "defeathered" without ceasing to be Indian.

Contemporary Issues
and Concerns

Chapter **6**

Signs of self-confidence and self-assertion among Canadian Indians in the last two or three decades abound. Many men and women are taking roles as leaders and participants in Indian communities, on and off reserves, in organizations, in the communications media and in many other aspects of Indian life.

Status and non-status Indians are numerically on the increase. Their population, despite high infant mortality and shorter life expectancy than Canadian averages, is growing rapidly, at a rate well above that of the nation as a whole.

The City and the Reserve

Many reserves are no longer able to contain and employ their residents. Perhaps as many as one-third of the people now live off reserves through much of the year, and most of these are moving to the cities. They are thus not only more numerous but more noticeable than they were fifty years ago. The "vanishing red men" of the nineteenth century are no longer vanishing.

The reserves have not proved to be training grounds for total assimilation. Adaptation and adjustment are still taking place, but the Indians are seeking ways to increase their control over the changes which occur. Greater self-government on reserves is one means to this end, and local reserve governments are pressing for greater authority over their own affairs. Control of finances and the power to make and enforce decisions are key goals. In the two northern territories the majority of the people are Indians, Métis and non-status Indians, and Inuit. Natives in those two areas hope the time will come when provincial governments will be created. In that case community and provincial governments may reflect the cultures and concerns of their native majorities.

Pauline Johnson (1861-1913) gained international fame for her poems, which celebrated nature and the Indian people. She once wrote "There are those who think they pay me a compliment in saying I am just like a white woman. I am an Indian, and my aim, my joy, my pride, is to sing the glories of my people."

A New History

The Indians' desire for greater self-government is accompanied by a desire for greater knowledge about their past. Most of the accounts of Indian history have been written by non-Indians and are based on non-Indian sources. Indians have been pictured as the enemy or as backward people to be used and discarded or changed and made over. They have been written about mostly in terms of their contribution to the history of the newcomers.

Exploration, the fur trade and wars are the most familiar contexts in which they are discussed. Until recently Indian sources have been largely ignored by scholars except in the field of anthropology. History is usually reconstructed from written sources and Canadian Indians did not have writing. As a result, Indians believe, distortion and error fill the historical accounts and must be corrected. One way of correcting these inaccuracies is to include more from the traditions of the Indians—the Indian side of the story. This means giving more importance to what has been remembered and passed on by word of mouth, to oral traditions.

Much of the study of Indians has centered on the things they used and made—canoes, tipis, feather bonnets, moccassins, totem poles. These artifacts tell much about the old culture, but Indians also stress the importance of beliefs, values, religion. In order to understand Indian history greater attention must be given to these aspects of Indian culture. Indian history must be rewritten, then, so that it will be more accurate and more balanced, and this revised history must be made available to both Indians and non-Indians.

Indians often feel that existing historical accounts portray them in negative and destructive ways which are both untrue and harmful. It is hoped that rediscovering the past will, by presenting a more balanced picture, contribute to a new pride among Indians and to a better understanding between Indians and non-Indians. In this way Indian rebirth, or resurgence, or renaissance (all of the terms have been used) includes greater control of their understanding and interpretation of their past as well as greater control of plans and actions for their future.

Seeking Change

Since 1876 the major legislation governing Indian life has been the Indian Act. It defines who is an Indian and sets out the rules which control Indian communities. Contemporary Indians would like to see changes in the Indian Act. Legislation which is so important to their lives, they argue, should reflect their attitudes and viewpoints. If there is to be an Indian Act, it should be of their design, not imposed on them by others unfamiliar with their needs and interests.

Reserves are the last homelands of status Indians. They are what was left after most of the Indians' land had been taken from them—whether by treaties or without treaties. They are Indian communities where traditions and customs may be kept alive. Some of the reserves are several thousand acres, but many are quite small. A large number of Indian communities are finding that reserve lands are not adequate to support their growing populations. Nevertheless they are unwilling to have reserves abolished because this would mean the loss of the last bits of their native land and the disruption of the continuity of their native communities.

Employment for people on reserves is an important issue. Efforts are being made to improve existing jobs and to create new ones. Ranching, mining, logging, fishing and farming are occupations long practised on many reserves; industry and tourism are two new forms of economic expansion being tried by some bands for their reserves. The growth of large cities near reserves has helped in some cases by creating jobs to which Indians can commute.

Health and housing standards on the reserves are a major concern as they have been for a very long time. The new strength of Indian voices has been directed towards improving living conditions. Running water, electricity, indoor plumbing, sewage systems, paved streets, hospitals and clinics are often needed to bring reserve standards up to the standards of other Canadian communities. Often public opinion must be aroused among both Indians and non-Indians in order to get the necessary improvements. Indian reserve governments and Indian organizations are making effective use of the communications media to call attention to their needs, and efforts are being made to raise their living standards.

Nonetheless, some people are leaving the reserves, temporarily or for a lifetime. Indians and other native people are moving into cities in increasing numbers. Estimates are that tens of thousands of Indians and Métis now reside, more or less permanently, in cities like Toronto, Edmonton, Vancouver, Winnipeg. In some smaller cities, such as Regina and Saskatoon, they may already constitute 25 percent of the population. Many of these people are unskilled labourers and inexperienced in urban living. They face unemployment and a sense of dislocation.

The reserves are small communities, slower paced, often seasonal in their work patterns. The reserve is where the people know everyone and are known; many if not most of the people on a reserve are kinfolk. The Indian language is often still spoken there. Food supplies may be supplemented by hunting and fishing. In the city all or most of these elements are missing. The city is "foreign" territory, with different customs and ways from those of the reserve. At the same time, for those who can find employment and make the adjustment, the city can mean higher wages, better housing, better schools, more labour-saving appliances and amenities. It can mean the entertainments and attractions which the Indian has learned about at school and from tele-

The oil industry has provided jobs for many Alberta Indians, sometimes right on their own reserves.

vision, radio, newspapers, magazines, movies and from the accounts of those who have gone to the cities before them.

The city also challenges their imagination to find a way to continue being Indians. Indian culture evolved among hunters, fishers and gatherers living by the natural fruits of land and sea. The people lived in small units with values and traditions that had been developed to suit their needs. Indians must now try to fit these values and traditions into an urban way of life in order to preserve continuity with the different life of the older culture.

In the city Indians of several tribes and traditions mix, and while they recognize differences, they are also trying to develop a common sense of Indianness. Clubs, associations, friendship centres and other organizations offer assistance in adjusting to city life and help people to preserve their Indian identity. In Ontario in the early 1980s, there were five Indian organizations representing the interests of reserve Indians, two representing off-reserve (mostly towns and cities) interests, and one representing both reserve and off-reserve interests of status and non-status Indians. These were in addition to federal and provincial agencies dealing with native people.

Charles Edenshaw (1839-1920), master Haida carver, photographed with the kind of carvings that made him famous. He worked mainly in wood and argillite, a scarce, slate-like rock found in the Queen Charlotte Islands which acquires a satiny black sheen when cut and polished. The family carving tradition has been carried on by his nephew Charles Gladstone and by the latter's grandson, Bill Reid.

The various Indian organizations maintain programs which deal with Indian concerns, including health, education, treaties, the Indian Act, recreation, housing, community development, Indian women and the Indian and the law. They sponsor study groups, research workshops, newspapers and recreational activities. Religious and social ceremonies and rituals are carried on, and there has been in the last two decades or so an outpouring of native Indian and Inuit art in a variety of media, including sculpture, painting and drawing.

Artists

Across the country the cultural rebirth of Canadian Indians has produced artists of national and international reputation. Perhaps the best known of these is the Ontario Ojibwa artist Norval Morrisseau (Copper Thunderbird). Morrisseau combines subjects and ideas from traditional culture with contemporary techniques. His work began to be publicly exhibited in the 1960s. Previously he had for a long time argued with himself whether it was proper to paint and exhibit subjects which are of a private and religious nature. Eventually he had a vision in which divine permission was given. His paintings often show beings that combine animal and human elements and have supernatural qualities and powers.

Morrisseau has influenced, directly or indirectly, other Indian artists of eastern Canada. Like Morrisseau they use traditional themes, stories, beliefs and render them in their own personal styles. Francis Kagige, Carl Ray and Benjamin Chee-Chee each developed unique styles while drawing upon their Ojibwa or Cree backgrounds. An important function of aboriginal art was its representation of and use in religious and supernatural activities. Many modern Indian artists illustrate this tradition.

West Coast art is best seen in the wood carving of the so-called totem poles. Its traditions have been revived under the direction and instruction of older carvers. Mungo Martin, a Kwakiutl and one of the best-known of the West Coast carvers, trained several younger men to continue this art form. After decades of neglect, pole-carving and the raising of poles are again taking place. Craftspeople learn to use both traditional and modern tools. Stone sculpture, another West Coast tradition, has been continued and given commercial importance in the form of jewelry and small art objects. The continuity in this tradition is perhaps best illustrated by the prominence of artist Bill Reid, a Haida, whose ancestors, the Edenshaws, were widely recognized carvers generations ago.

The prairie provinces have also produced Indian artists, including Alex Janvier, Alan Sapp, and Jackson Beardy. These artists work in a variety of styles such as contemporary abstract forms, representational forms and forms adapted from traditional art.

The Indian Pavilion at Expo 67, the World's Fair held in Montreal during Canada's centennial year, made Canadians more aware of Indian art and the survival of Indian crafts. By calling attention to this aspect of modern Indian culture, it provided encouragement and stimulated markets for the work of Indian artists and craftspeople.

Writers
Numerous Indian writers have begun to be published, especially since the debate over the 1969 Federal government White Paper

on Indians. Many Indian people saw the White Paper as a threat and reacted with books and research studies arguing against its proposals and making proposals of their own. Harold Cardinal's *The Unjust Society* was one of the first to appear. It described Indian conditions and outlined the origins of these conditions. Cardinal was the president of the Indian Association of Alberta and a leader in the National Indian Brotherhood.

Not all the books were concerned with public affairs, however. Books on Indian art and traditions also appeared. A book of essays and poetry entitled *The Only Good Indian*, edited by Waubageshig (Harvey McCue), of Trent University's Native Studies Program, was published in 1970. Wilf Pelletier, of Manitoulin Island, wrote on Indian life and values in his autobiography, *No Foreign Land*.

Performing Artists and Film-Makers
Duke Redbird wrote, directed and acted in films about Indians. Indian popular singers such as Buffy Sainte-Marie and Willie Dunn reach wide audiences with their songs, many of them on Indian themes. Several Canadian Indians, including Nootka artist George Clutesi (who has also written children's books retelling Indian oral traditions) have developed acting careers. The most prominent among them was Chief Dan George of North Vancouver, British Columbia, who also gained a reputation as a moving speaker and writer. One of the first Ontario Indians to be a successful movie and television actor before the resurgence of the last two decades or so was Jay Silverheels who played Tonto, friend of The Lone Ranger.

Politicians
Another example of the Indians' resurgence is their increased participation in provincial and federal politics. In 1960 status Indians were granted the right to vote in federal elections. They had previously voted in a few provinces and now can vote in all. British Columbia became the first province to have an Indian member of the Legislative Assembly, Frank Calder, a Nishga, in the mid-1950s. Later Mr. Calder was the first Indian cabinet minister.

Prime Minister John Diefenbaker appointed James Gladstone, an Alberta Blackfoot, to be the first Indian senator. After

Gladstone's death a prominent British Columbia Indian figure, Guy Williams, went to the Senate. Since then Len Marchand, a member of Parliament from British Columbia was a federal cabinet minister. Wally Firth, a non-status Indian, sat as member of Parliament for the Northwest Territories in the 1970s. As we have already noted, many of the members of the territorial legislatures are status and non-status Indians.

Native Rights

Indians and Indian organizations were very prominent in the public debate in 1980-81 on the patriation of the British North America Act and the reforms introduced into the constitution. They have achieved greater skills and influence in their dealings with the federal government, both with the ministry in charge of Indian administration and with others.

Native rights, especially land rights, have been one of the most important topics dealt with between the federal government and the various Indian organizations. Indians claim rights in the land because of their aboriginal status, that is their earlier occupancy and ownership. In those provinces and territories where

Elementary school children at Curve Lake Ojibwa Reserve in Ontario.

Indian artist Gerald Tailfeathers juxtaposes the old and the new in his painting Blood Camps.

treaties were never made, settlements are called for. These require much research, study and negotiation. Indians are pressing their claims. In other parts of Canada, though treaties surrendering the land were made, Indians call attention to unfulfilled agreements within the treaties. Sometimes these are clear agreements, but sometimes they are subject to different interpretations. Sometimes the written agreement differs from remembered oral agreements. Complicated negotiations and decisions, extensive research and examination are necessary to settle these questions.

Hunting and fishing rights are another important issue. For a time the Indians were allowed to continue hunting and fishing throughout most of the lands surrendered by treaty. This changed, however, as settlers came in, and Indians found themselves prevented from following their earlier ways of gaining their livelihood. Later, conservation laws were often passed which placed restrictions on the taking of wild game, and international agreements were made to protect and shelter certain species of wildlife. Any or all of these forms of control might place further limitations on the Indians without consultation with or agreement by them. If these laws are interpreted as applying to reserves, Indians resist their enforcement. This sometimes leads to arrests and protests. More recently pollution of streams, lakes and the ocean has affected fishing. Although the fish are there to be taken, they are contaminated. Indians protest these developments as examples of the loss of rights which they have claimed or which were specifically granted by treaties, court rulings and administrative decisions.

Two additional social issues of concern are the status of Indian women and education for Indians. Indian status is not entirely a matter of race; it is a legal determination. Under the Indian Act of 1876 an Indian woman who married a non-Indian lost her status as an Indian. Her name would be removed from her band list, or roll, and she would cease to be legally a member of the band and a status Indian. Moreover, even if she was later divorced or widowed, she could not regain her Indian status. The Act made no such provision in the case of an Indian man who married a non-Indian. On the contrary, the non-Indian wife of an Indian gained Indian status. The children of the woman who married a non-Indian did not have Indian status either, whereas the children of the Indian man who married a non-status woman were Indians under the law. A number of Indian women—and others—have regarded this aspect of the Indian Act as very discriminatory and have actively sought to have it changed. Many Indians, however, foresaw a variety of problems, such as overcrowding of reserves or non-Indians getting control of reserve lands, resulting from the removal of this provision. It therefore remained virtually intact into the early 1980s in spite of the government's expressed willingness to alter it. Although it is possible in other ways to give up one's Indian status, most Indians who have lost it are women who have had it taken away by marrying a non-Indian.

Education
Education for Indians, especially on reserves but also in urban communities with large numbers of Indians is another matter of great concern. This is related to the efforts to provide links with

the past and, at the same time, the skills and knowledge that will allow Indians to adapt to the changing world of the future. Indians desire to have greater control over the subjects taught in their schools, the books and materials used, the qualifications of the teachers and teachers' assistants. The use and teaching of Indian languages in the schools is also an aspect of the issue.

In some communities in the North, Cree or Chipewyan or another Indian language may be the main or only language the children know. In such cases schools are being called for which will use both English and the Indian language. The latter would be the language of beginning instruction, and a shift to English would be made in higher grades.

In other communities the native language is not spoken much, but there is a desire to restore it to greater use, and the schools can be part of this effort. Both kinds of communities require teachers who can speak the local Indian language. In the early 1980s there was still a shortage of Indians who had the usual teacher training and diplomas. Adaptations and adjustments are sought to deal with these situations.

Federal Indian policy now encourages Indian control of Indian education. Indian-run schools and school boards are necessary to define the educational needs of the Indian communities and to satisfy these needs. Urbanized Indians are meeting some of these concerns by having language classes at friendship centres and through other voluntary associations. In cities such as Toronto where Indians form large minorities, Indian studies, including that of Indian languages, are being called for and introduced.

Prejudice and discrimination continue to be reported by native peoples at work and in school. Indians see the ending of this situation as a long-term educational process.

Variety and Diversity
Variety and diversity are themes often emphasized in Canada as desirable, as preferable to uniformity and forced sameness. The Indians in their aboriginal lives had variety and diversity in their cultures. Although there were similarities and resemblances, different languages, dress, customs, religion, ways of making a living were the rule. Before the coming of the Europeans there were

no "Indians," but there were many "peoples." Today Indians, like other Canadians, combine unity and diversity. They have made and are making a variety of adjustments. Many are going into cities or live on reserves near urban centres and are successfully making the transition to the life of the urban industrial society. Many others prefer the life of the rural reserve, working in tourist industries, ranching, logging, hunting, fishing. The Hurons of Lorette, Quebec, manufacture sports equipment; the Nishga and other West Coast Indians use the most modern ships and techniques to fish; Chief Robert Smallboy has led a band of Cree to try to re-adapt to living off the land.

In effect Indians are diversifying their ways of life in the new conditions as they have been doing since they first came to this land thousands, probably tens of thousands, of years ago.

Selected Biographies

AHENAKEW, Edward (1885-1961)

Edward Ahenakew, a Plains Cree, was born in 1885 on the Sandy Lake reserve, Saskatchewan. This was the reserve of Ah-Tah-Ka-Koop (Star-blanket), a kinsman of his. As a young man Ahenakew became a teacher and later an Anglican priest (1912) on various reserves in Saskatchewan. He studied medicine for a time, but ill health forced him to give it up. His scholarly interests led him to study and write on the life of Big Bear. His book *Voices of the Plains Cree* describes life on the reserve at the turn of the century and the efforts of his people to adapt to western civilization. He also compiled a Cree-English dictionary and collected legends and stories.

In the 1920s and 1930s Ahenakew was active in forming Indian organizations in Saskatchewan and nationally. He served as honorary provincial president of the League of Indians of Canada and was awarded a Doctor of Divinity degree (1947). Ahenakew's career illustrates the efforts of the Cree to select what was best from European culture while retaining what was best of their own.

BRANT, Joseph (Thayendanegea) (1742-1807)

Joseph Brant was born in the Ohio Valley, but his parents returned a few years later to their home in the Mohawk country of New York. He came to manhood at a time when the Mohawks, and the Six Nations of the Iroquois generally, were feeling the pressures of the growing numbers of European settlers and the rivalries of the French and British empires. The Mohawks were allies of the British, and Brant began his career as a warrior at the age of thirteen.

From 1761 to 1763 Brant attended Moor's Indian School in Lebanon, Connecticut. Under a schoolmaster whose goal was to make Englishmen of his pupils, he learned English, became acquainted with English literature and history and converted to Christianity. When he left the school he became interpreter to a missionary and then interpreter and assistant to Sir William Johnson, the British superintendent for northern Indians. During the American Revolution Brant led Indian loyalist forces and sought to gain additional Indian allies.

After the war Brant led some of the loyalist Indians (sometimes referred to as "feathered loyalists") to Canada. He became their spokesman in the land settlement negotiations for the control and use of the huge grant made to the Iroquois on the Grand River.

While continuing to act as leader of his people, Brant did missionary work, wrote several religious books and translated into Mohawk part of the New Testament and the Anglican Prayer Book. His home was a centre of social as well as administrative and business affairs until his death in November 1807.

CROWFOOT (c. 1830-1890)

Crowfoot was born into the Blood tribe of the Blackfoot Confederacy. His mother married into the Blackfoot tribe and he grew up in the band of his stepfather, Many Names, learning to ride, hunt and raid for horses and for prestige. He took the name Crowfoot after an especially heroic performance during a raid into Montana. In 1865 he became the Chief of a small, newly formed band, the Big Pipes. His reputation for courage and good leadership caused his band to grow, and by the early 1870s he had become a major chief of the Blackfoot.

Throughout his years as chief, Crowfoot counselled peace both among tribes and between Indians and non-Indians. In order to end the tradition of war between Blackfoot and Cree, he adopted Cree Chief Poundmaker as his son. In 1877, in the interest of the peace and welfare of his people, he signed Treaty Number Seven and influenced other Blackfoot leaders to do so. His influence kept the Blackfoot out of the Riel uprising of 1885. Crowfoot used his tact and prestige to preserve harmony on his reserve when food shortages developed and friction occurred between Indians and employees of the Indian Administration. His most important contribution was aiding the peaceful adaptation of his people to a new life.

DUMONT, GABRIEL (1838-1906)
Gabriel Dumont was born at Red River of Métis parents. He grew up without formal education but quickly acquired a reputation as a shrewd buffalo hunter and a brave fighting man.

Although he took no part in the 1870 uprising, Dumont moved soon afterwards to the Batoche area on the banks of the Saskatchewan River. He became head of the Métis community there and organized the great buffalo hunts. In 1884 he was one of the delegates who persuaded Louis Riel to come back to the Canadian Northwest.

Dumont commanded the Métis forces during the rebellion of 1885. He was an excellent strategist but his "army" was hopelessly outnumbered once the government troops arrived. After the defeat at Batoche, he fled to the United States and lived there for several years, appearing in Buffalo Bill's Wild West Show. He eventually returned to Canada when the Canadian government granted him an amnesty.

GRANT, Cuthbert (1793-1854)
Cuthbert Grant was born at Fort Tremblant, in present-day Saskatchewan, the second son of a Scottish North West Company officer and his Cree wife. He was educated in Scotland and Montreal and became a clerk in the North West Company at the age of nineteen. When he was sent to the Red River area, his education, family connections and ability quickly made him a leader of the Métis. Encouraged by the North West Company, the Métis opposed the Selkirk settlers. Several clashes occurred, including the battle of Seven Oaks (1816) in which Grant led the Métis force. He was arrested and imprisoned in Quebec City in 1817, but he either escaped or was released the following year and returned to the West.

When the Hudson's Bay and North West companies merged, Grant did not get an appointment, though he was hired briefly between 1822-1824. During this time he became a friend of Governor George Simpson and placed his ability and influence at the company's disposal. He was given a grant of land on the Assiniboine River and founded Grantown, a settlement of fifty or more

Métis families. In 1828 the Company named him "Warden of the Plains" and he later became sheriff and magistrate as well as a member of the Council of Assiniboia. He maintained these positions until his accidental death in 1854.

JOHNSTON, Verna Patronella (1900-   )

Verna Johnston was born on the Cape Croker reserve where her ancestors were of Ojibwa, Potawatomi and European origins. Her father, Peter Nadjiwon, served in World War I for three years (1915-1918). She married Henry Johnston in 1926 and raised five children. After they were grown she moved to Toronto for a time, then returned to the reserve.

Many Indians were going to cities to find jobs, schooling and a better life. Mrs. Johnston returned to Toronto in 1966 and opened a boarding house to assist some of these people. She became very familiar with the problems people faced in learning to adjust from the life of the reserve to that of the large city. In 1970 she wrote a book, *Tales of Nokomis*, which tells traditional stories of the Ojibwa. Nokomis was the wise woman whose counsel and knowledge gave support to human life.

After one more return to the reserve, Mrs. Johnston went to work at Anduhyuan House, an Indian centre in Toronto, where she acted as housekeeper and counsellor. She remembers the teachings of the elders, and in her turn she teaches the traditional crafts and stories. In this way native culture is passed on to the urbanized Indians who wish to retain contact with their roots.

In 1976 Verna Johnston was named Indian Woman of the Year by the Native Women's Association of Canada. She has herself become a *Nokomis*, a wise woman whose advice and lore enriches the lives of others.

MORRISSEAU, Norval (1931-   )

Norval Morrisseau, one of Canada's most influential artists, was born in Fort William, Ontario. His grandmother was a devout Roman Catholic and his grandfather kept the traditional religious beliefs of the Ojibwa. These two influences gave him a rich spiritual life and filled his mind with religious images. As a child he lived on the shores of Lake Nipigon until he was sent to boarding school in Thunder Bay, where he stayed for six years. After more time in a public school in Beardmore, Ontario, he returned to his family and began to paint. His grandfather showed him how to make pictures on birchbark like those used in the Midewiwin.

Some people thought it was wrong for Morrisseau to paint these sacred images for public exhibition. He himself had doubts at first, but a dream assured him that he was permitted to do so. In 1962, the Toronto art dealer, Jack Pollock, arranged for exhibitions of his work. At this time Morrisseau's paintings were in black and shades of warm brown on paper. They showed the manitous, the demigods of the Ojibwa: Mikkimuk, the turtle; Mishipeshu, the Water Lynx. These works were very successful and most of them were sold.

Morrisseau's style continued to develop. He began adding bright colours, painting in acrylics on canvas and designing silk screen prints. His later works are as brilliant as stained glass windows. In all of them, the spiritual world remains his subject. He has created large murals for public buildings, and his works now hang in major collections all over Canada. A new generation of Indian painters has followed his direction, creating beautiful works of art from the vision images of Algonkian religion.

PAULL, Andrew (1892-1959)

As a child Andrew Paull moved with his family to Mission Reserve #1, North Vancouver. There he was educated by Sister Hieronymie of the Sisters of the Child Jesus. He considered becoming a priest, but chose instead to involve himself in Indian public affairs. He was secretary to his band and was active in inviting the various Squamish bands into a tribal government. His knowledge of provincial affairs grew when he acted as interpreter for a Royal Commission (1913-1916) on Indian land claims in British Columbia.

In the 1920s Paull helped to organize Indian longshoremen and later he was a key figure in organizing native fishermen on Vancouver Island. In 1942 he joined the Native Brotherhood of British Columbia and became its business manager.

Paull wanted to expand his own area of activity and to bring all Canadian Indians together. This led him in 1944 to form the North American Indian Brotherhood. The organization took a strong watchdog role in Indian affairs, the kind of role Paull had personally taken for many years. Despite failing health and blindness, Paull continued to be active until his death in a Vancouver hospital in 1959. His career made him an important forerunner of many of today's Indian leaders.

POUNDMAKER (1842-1886)

Poundmaker was a Plains Cree Indian who grew up in the traditional culture of his buffalo-hunting people. He came from a family of outstanding leaders, including the original Poundmaker for whom he was named. As a young man he was adopted by the Blackfoot chief Crowfoot. Both he and Crowfoot saw the importance of ending the long tradition of war between Cree and Blackfoot.

Poundmaker became chief after his people had signed Treaty Number Six in 1876. His reputation for integrity and leadership resulted in his being asked to accompany the Governor General of Canada, the Marquis of Lorne, during his tour of the Northwest in 1881.

As the buffalo declined, Poundmaker led his band to accept life on a reserve and to attempt to farm the land. Here again he showed his ability to adapt to a new and unusual situation, for the Cree had never in all their existence been farmers.

Discontent grew among the Cree in the early 1800s, however, and in 1885 Poundmaker and his band joined the uprising led by Louis Riel. Poundmaker fought brilliantly, but with the defeat of Riel he was forced to surrender. Although he had rebuked his young men for looting and burning at Battleford and had allowed the government troops to escape annihilation at Cut Knife Hill, he was tried and convicted of treason. He was sentenced to three years in prison but was not forced to cut his long braids and was released after nine months through the intervention of his adoptive father, Crowfoot.

Poundmaker died shortly after his release. Defeat and imprisonment had broken his health. He had attempted to defend his people and acted with humanity and restraint even while under arms.

RIEL, Louis (1844-1885)

Louis Riel was the son of a Métis father and of Julie Lagimodière, daughter of the first white woman in the West. His family was prominent in the public life of the Red River Colony and he was singled out for an education in Montreal. In 1868 he returned to the Red River area and soon became a leader in the Métis protest over the transfer of Rupert's Land from the Hudson's Bay Company to the government of Canada. Because of his education, his personal magnetism and his family, Riel was well suited to lead the protest. In early 1870 a provisional government, under Riel's presidency, negotiated with Ottawa the terms under which the colony would accept the transfer. These included provincial status, equality for the French and English languages and treaties with the Indians. Most of Riel's "list of rights" were included in the Manitoba Act (May 1870).

Riel, however, was accused of murder and a warrant for his arrest was issued. Though elected to Parliament, he was not able to take his seat. He became a fugitive and eventually his mental health broke down. After spending most of 1876-78 in insane asylums in Quebec, he settled in Montana, where he became active in the Métis community and taught school.

In June 1884 the Métis of the Saskatchewan Valley asked him to return to Canada to lead the Métis there in their protest against the Canadian government's indifference to their grievances. Once again, they felt, the civilization of eastern, English-speaking Canada was threatening the "New Nation." Fighting broke out in March, 1885. At first, the victories went to the Métis and their Indian allies, but this quickly changed when troops were brought in on the new railway line. The rebellion was quickly crushed and Riel was tried and convicted of treason. He was hanged in Regina on November 16, 1885.

SHANAWDITHIT (c. 1805-1829)

To the best of anyone's knowledge, Shanawdithit, also known as Nancy April, was the last Beothuk Indian. She grew up in the River of Exploits area of central Newfoundland where her family lived by hunting, fishing and gathering.

In April 1823, when she was eighteen or nineteen, Shanawdithit was taken captive with her mother and older sister. They both died not long afterwards of tuberculosis, and Shanawdithit continued to live at Exploits, Newfoundland, with the John Peyton family. She learned English and was found to be well informed about Beothuk culture. Scholars interested in this subject heard of her, and in 1828 she was taken to St. John's. She was able to tell them a great deal about Beothuk life, customs and material culture, and this was recorded at the Beothuk Institute. She also had a remarkable natural artistic skill and made drawings which illustrated the life of her people.

In 1829, at the age of about twenty-five, Shanadithit died of tuberculosis.

TECUMSEH (c. 1768-1813)

The son of a Shawnee chief, Tecumseh was born near what is now Springfield, Ohio. When he was about six, his father was killed by an American, and he grew up hating the American settlers who were taking over Indian lands and fearing their influence on Indian culture.

After years of fighting against American troops and settlers, Tecumseh settled in Indiana with his brother Tenskwatawa, known as "the Prophet." From there he began trying to organize the Indian tribes into a vast alliance that could more successfully resist the pressure from the settlers and the American government. He made long journeys urging resistance and winning supporters. While he was on one of his trips, however, Indians led by the Prophet were drawn into battle with American troops and badly defeated.

Still hoping to stem the tide of American advance, Tecumseh and his followers fought on the side of the British in the War of 1812. They played a major role in the capture of Detroit early in the war. Tecumseh led the Indians with great courage until he was killed in the battle of the Thames on October 5, 1813.

TEKAKWITHA, Kateri (1656-1680)

Kateri Tekakwitha was born at Gandaouague on the Mohawk River in eastern New York. Her mother was a Christian Algonkian Indian from Three Rivers, Quebec, and her father a Mohawk. At the age of four she was struck with smallpox. Though she survived, her eyesight was impaired and her face left scarred. Her parents died in the epidemic and she was adopted by an uncle and aunt. She grew up a model of young Iroquois womanhood, learning the skills necessary for her adult life.

At the age of nineteen, apparently following a long-developing interest, Tekakwitha became a convert to Christianity. She was baptized on Easter Sunday, 1676. In her circumstances this was extremely unusual, and she found it difficult to live as a Christian in a traditionalist Mohawk village. In 1677 she fled to the mission of Saint-François-Xavier near Montreal. Although she was misunderstood and even persecuted at first, she gradually gained a reputation for great piety and devotion. Following the practices of fasting and self-mortification that were a major aspect of seventeenth-century French piety, she ruined her health, which had never been strong, and died at the age of twenty-four.

Tekakwitha's unusual and saintly life captured the imagination of many non-Indian Roman Catholics. She came to be known as the Lily of the Mohawks, and numerous cures and other favours were attributed to her intercession. On June 22, 1980 she was beatified, that is declared to be among the blessed in heaven, by Pope John Paul II.

Glossary

Aboriginal   Relating to the earliest known inhabitants of a place. "Aboriginal rights" refer to the right of native people to the lands they occupied before the establishment of the Dominion of Canada.

Anthropology   The scientific study of the origins and development of human beings and human culture.

Archaeologist   A scientist who searches for and studies material evidence remaining from human life and culture in past ages.

Artifact   An object made by human workmanship, and particularly one such as a simple tool, weapon or ornament which is of archaeological or historical interest.

Band   A group of Indians recognized by the federal government as an administrative unit. It includes all and only members of the group who are officially registered as such. Although a band is usually identified with a particular reserve, it is not necessary to live on the reserve to be a band member.

Confederacy   A union or alliance of countries or groups of people.

Culture   The way of life of a people. It includes everything a group of people has, makes, thinks, believes and passes on to its children.

Ethnic   Refers to a group within a society that share certain cultural traits, usually including ancestry and language and sometimes religion.

Métis   In this book, the term *Métis* has been used to refer to the people of mixed Indian and non-Indian race who developed their sense of identity in the Red River Colony in the early nineteenth century. In recent years the term, which means mixed, has come to be used more generally for any or all persons of mixed Indian and non-Indian blood, without reference to the nation which developed out of the Red River Colony.

Midden   A mound containing shells, bones and other refuse that accumulated at places where prehistoric people lived.

Nation   See **Tribe**

Pemmican   Dried meat pounded into a paste and mixed with melted fat. Made from buffalo meat on the Prairies and from moose meat in more northern regions, pemmican was concentrated and nutritious and would keep for long periods of time.

Potlatch A ceremony held by wealthy West Coast Indians to mark an important change or event in their lives. The main feature of the ceremony was lavish gift-giving by the holder of the potlatch. The word *potlatch*, in fact, means "to give."

Prehistoric Belonging to the time before there were written records. Since the Indians had no writing, the term is used for their entire past up to the arrival of the Europeans. The expression historic times refers to the period after Indian-European contact.

Reserve Tract of land set aside for the exclusive use of a specific band of Indians.

Scurvy A disease caused by a lack of vitamin C in the diet and characterized by weakness, swollen and bleeding gums and spots on the skin. To cure it, the Indians used the crushed, boiled leaves and bark of an evergreen tree.

Status Legal position. To have Indian status is to be classified as an Indian under the terms of the Indian Act. This means being registered as a member of a specific band. A non-status Indian is a person who is not registered and not legally considered to be an Indian. Some non-status Indians are Indians or descendants of Indians who gave up their status. Others are descendants of Indians who somehow were simply never registered as such. Many are Indian women who married non-Indians and their children.

Totem A natural object, often an animal or bird, taken as the emblem of a tribe, clan or family. The members of some West Coast tribes carved and painted their totems on tall "totem poles" which they raised outside their dwellings.

Treaty A formal agreement between countries or people. There were many kinds of treaties—peace, trade, alliance—but those of greatest importance in the context of this book are the treaties by which many Indians surrendered most of their land in return for some kind of payment.

Tribe This is a term which has been commonly used by many different people over a long period and which has many meanings. It may be used as the equivalent of *nation*, as in "the Ojibwa tribe," or it may refer to a subgroup, as in "the Tsimshian tribes" or "the tribes of the Huron Confederacy." The term *nation* can be used for groups which have also been called tribes, as in "the Six Nations of the Iroquois," but it may also refer to a larger grouping containing more than one "tribe," as in "the Dene nation."

Selected Further Reading

The Canadians. Toronto: Fitzhenry and Whiteside. This series of short biographies includes the lives of Joseph Brant, Crowfoot, Poundmaker, Gabriel Dumont and Louis Riel.

Dewdney, Selwyn. *They Shared to Survive.* Toronto: Macmillan, 1975. A description of native lifestyles and the impact of European culture upon them.

Embree, Jesse. *Let Us Live.* Toronto: J. M. Dent and Sons, 1977. A short, well-illustrated introduction to native life today and in Canadian history.

Ginn Studies in Canadian History. Toronto: Ginn and Company. This clearly-written and colourfully-illustrated series includes booklets on several Indian groups.

Gooderham, Kent, ed. *I Am an Indian.* Toronto: J. M. Dent and Sons, 1969. An anthology of stories, poems and other writings by Canadian Indians.

Harris, Christie. *Raven's Cry.* Toronto: McClelland and Stewart, 1966. Bill Reid, a descendant of Haida chiefs, illustrated this novelized account of the tragic destruction of a proud people.

Jenness, Diamond. *Indians of Canada, 7th ed.* Toronto: University of Toronto Press, 1977. First published in 1932, this remains the standard reference work on Canada's original peoples.

Morrisseau, Norval. *Legends of My People: The Great Ojibway.* Toronto: McGraw-Hill Ryerson, 1965. The famous Ojibwa artist illustrates his own account of the beliefs and legends of his people.

Patterson, Nancy-Lou. *Canadian Native Art.* Toronto: Collier-Macmillan, 1973. A study of native arts and crafts presented as part of everyday life.

Rodgers, Edward S. *Indians of Canada.* Toronto: Royal Ontario Museum, 1970. Series of six illustrated booklets discussing the Indians' way of life in the major geographical regions of the country.

Sealy, Donald Bruce and Lussier, Antoine S. *The Métis: Canada's Forgotten People.* Winnipeg: Manitoba Métis Federation Press, 1975. A comprehensive and straightforward history of the Métis.

Surtees, Robert J. *The Original People.* Toronto: Holt, Rhinehart and Winston, 1971. A good, general introduction with emphasis on past relationships between Indians and the government.

Symington, Fraser. *The First Canadians.* Toronto: Natural Science of Canada, 1978 (Canada's Illustrated Heritage). This profusely illustrated book provides a wealth of information on how the various culture groups lived before the arrival of the Europeans.

Theriault, Yves. *Ashini.* Montreal: Harvest House, 1972. A novel about the last Montagnais chief to live according to the ancient customs of his people.

Updike, Lee R. and Symons, R. D. *The First People: An Artist's Reconstruction of Five Native Canadian Cultures.* Saskatoon: Western Producer Prairie Books, 1978. Glimpses into the day-to-day life of native peoples.

Willis, Jane. *Geneish: An Indian Girlhood.* Toronto: New Press, 1973. A Cree from the eastern shore of James Bay tells of her childhood and her unhappy years in an Anglican boarding school.

For Discussion

CHAPTER 1

1) How did the majority of Canadian Indians make their living throughout most of their past?
2) What does "nomadic" mean? Why were most Indian tribes nomadic?
3) Some Canadian Indians cultivated the land. Who were they and where did they live? What effect did farming have on their way of life?
4) What made it possible for the West Coast peoples to live more like the agricultural groups than like other hunting and gathering groups?
5) Why was it necessary and desirable for Indians to share their goods and possessions?
6) Why was it important for a hunter or craftsperson to be religious?
7) What ceremonial objects and activities were common among Indians?
8) Name some ceremonial objects and activities common in Canadian society today. What ceremonial objects and activities have you observed?
9) What is meant by "culture areas"? What do you think are the main factors that led to the development of distinct cultures in these areas?
10) Read more about the way of life in one culture area. Write a report giving specific examples of features resulting directly from the above factors.

CHAPTER 2

1) Who were the Beothuk and what happened to them? Where does most of our information about them come from?
2) What Indian people who once lived in present-day Quebec seems to have disappeared between the 1540s and the early seventeenth century? What explanations have been offered to explain this?
3) What tribe dominated the fur trade in the Lower Great Lakes area in the early seventeenth century? Who were their Indian and non-Indian allies?
4) How did fur trade conflicts change the Indian population of what is now southern Ontario in the mid-seventeenth century?
5) Why were the Indians essential to the fur trade?
6) Imagine that you are Hurons living in 1640. Present and discuss the arguments for and against maintaining your tribe's trading alliance with the French.
7) Read more about Pontiac's uprising. Write a short essay outlining its causes and results.
8) What period is considered the "golden age" of the Plains Indians? Why?
9) Who are the Métis?
10) Imagine you are the fourteen-year-old Louis Riel recently sent to study at a school in Montreal. Describe for your new classmates what life was like back at Red River.
11) How might the government of Canada have avoided the 1870 Riel rebellion?

CHAPTER 3

1) A Micmac chief once spoke of the beaver as "making" all kinds of things. What did he mean? List some of the things he would have been referring to.
2) What was the major cause of population decline among many Indian tribes after the arrival of the Europeans?
3) What were some of the reasons several tribes shifted locations within a few decades of coming into contact with the Europeans?
4) Give some examples of cultural borrowing from one Indian group to another.
5) As the non-Indian population of Canada increased, the fur trade came to play a less and less important role in the total economy of the country. Why would this change make such a difference to the Indians?
6) Write an essay summarizing the effects of the fur trade on Indian Life.

CHAPTER 4

1) How did the increase in the number of white settlers put pressure on the Indians?
2) Explain with examples the distinction between voluntary change and involuntary change as experienced by the Indians.
3) "The reserve was meant to serve two major purposes at once." What were these?
4) How did the Indians' view of land differ from that of non-Indians? Explain how this led to misunderstanding.
5) In general, what did each side agree to in the treaties signed between the Indians and the government?
6) The Indians of the Prairies did not immediately settle on their reserves. What two major developments finally forced them to do so?
7) How did the pattern of Indian loss of their land in British Columbia differ from that in the Prairie Provinces and Ontario?
8) Why was the Indian Act passed?
9) What is meant by Indian status? Who has it?
10) Write a conversation that might have taken place between Poundmaker and Crowfoot on the question of whether or not to join the second Riel rebellion.
11) At least some of the Indians who signed the numbered treaties had a mistaken idea of what exactly was involved. If they had clearly understood what they were agreeing to, do you think they would have signed anyway? Why or why not?
12) The signing of the treaties usually included a great deal of speech making. Prepare a short speech that 1) a government representative might have made outlining the benefits of the treaty for the Indians; or 2) an Indian chief might have made expressing his view of the treaty.
13) Imagine that you are a missionary to the Hurons in the 1640s or at Metlakatla in the 1860s. Write a letter to your family explaining what you are trying to do and describing your life.
14) Canada did not go through the same kind of Indian wars as the United States did. Can you suggest reasons for this?

CHAPTER 5

1) Name two important twentieth century developments which affected Indian "rebirth" in Canada.
2) What factors contributed to the development of a sense of common, or Pan-Indian, identity?
3) Find out more about one of the Indian organizations mentioned in this chapter. Write a brief report on its aims and accomplishments.
4) What is meant by the "Fourth World"?
5) "Indian culture has much to offer non-Indians." Agree or disagree.

CHAPTER 6

1) Why do Indians feel that their history must be rewritten?
2) What are some of the main issues of concern to Indian organizations today?
3) Compare the advantages and disadvantages of life in a reserve community and life in the city.
4) Discuss: How can Indian culture(s) be kept alive among the increasing number of Indians who are moving to urban centres?
5) What does the upsurge in native artists, writers, actors tell us about Canadian Indians today?
6) Write a short biography of Chief Dan George, George Clutesi, Harold Cardinal or Buffy Sainte-Marie.
7) Make a survey of your neighbourhood. Do the people in it tend to have similar backgrounds and traditions or is it a mixed neighbourhood with different types of housing and people of different ethnic origins, income, religion and politics? Which kind of neighbourhood would you rather live in? Why?

THING TO DO

1) Visit a reserve.
2) Visit an Indian Friendship Centre in a city.
3) Invite an Indian speaker to your school.
4) Read books and stories by Indians.
5) Compare earlier and recent history books for their treatment of Indians.
6) Have a class discussion on your image of an Indian. What do you know about Indians? Do you know any Indians personally? Can you recognize Indians by appearance, dress, customs, language?

Index